Lord Palmerston

The Coalition Ministry, 1854. Lord Palmerston, at right, is seen pointing at the town of Balaclava on a map held open by the Duke of Newcastle.

Gregory A. Barton

Lord Palmerston
and the Empire of Trade

THE LIBRARY OF WORLD BIOGRAPHY

Edited by: Peter N. Stearns

Prentice Hall
Boston Columbus Indianapolis New York San Francisco Upper Saddle River
Amsterdam Cape Town Dubai London Madrid Milan Munich Paris Montréal Toronto
Delhi Mexico City São Paulo Sydney Hong Kong Seoul Singapore Taipei Tokyo

Editorial Director: Craig Campanella
Executive Editor: Jeff Lasser
Editorial Assistant: Julia Feltus
Senior Manufacturing and Operations Manager for Arts & Sciences: Nick Sklitsis
Operations Specialist: Clara Bartunek
Director of Marketing: Brandy Dawson
Senior Marketing Manager: Maureen E. Prado Roberts
Marketing Assistant: Marissa O'Brien
Senior Managing Editor: Ann Marie McCarthy
Senior Project Manager: Denise Forlow
Manager of Central Design: Jayne Conte
Cover Design: Karen Salzbach
Cover Image: The Print Collector, Great Britain / HIP / Art Resource, NY
AV Project Manager: Mirella Signoretto
Full-Service Production, Interior Design, and Composition: PreMediaGlobal
Printer / Binder: STP Courier / Stoughton
Text Font: Times New Roman

Library of Congress Cataloging-in-Publication Data
Barton, Greg (Gregory Allen)
  Lord Palmerston and the empire of trade / Gregory A. Barton.
     p. cm.
  Includes bibliographical references and index.
  ISBN-13: 978-0-321-39773-7
  ISBN-10: 0-321-39773-8
  1. Palmerston, Henry John Temple, Viscount, 1784-1865. 2. Prime ministers--Great Britain--Biography. 3. Great Britain--Politics and government--1837-1901. 4. Great Britain--Foreign relations--19th century. I. Title.
DA536.P2B37 2011
941.081092--dc22
[B]
                                        2010052055

Prentice Hall
is an imprint of

10 9 8 7 6 5 4 3 2 1

ISBN 10: 0-321-39773-8
ISBN 13: 978-0-321-39773-7

To Tad Stinson, my Victorian friend.

Contents

Editor's Preface		*vii*
Author's Preface		*viii*
Introduction		1
1	Palmerston's England	5
2	The People's Aristocrat	27
3	Palmerston the Canningite	50
4	Painting the Map Red	85
5	Palmerston and the World Britannica	117
A Note on the Sources		124
Brief Chronology		126
Index		128

Editor's Preface

"Biography is history seen through the prism of a person."

—Louis Fischer

It is often challenging to identify the roles and experiences of individuals in world history. Larger forces predominate. Yet biography provides important access to world history. It shows how individuals helped shape the society around them. Biography also offers concrete illustrations of larger patterns in political and intellectual life, in family life, and in the economy.

The Prentice Hall/Pearson Library of World Biography series seeks to capture the individuality and drama that mark human character. It deals with individuals operating in one of the main periods of world history, while also reflecting issues in the particular society around them. Here, the individual illustrates larger themes of time and place. The interplay between the personal and general is always the key to using biography in history, and world history is no exception. Always, too, there is the question of personal agency: how much do individuals, even great ones, shape their own lives and environment, and how much are they shaped by the world around them?

Peter N. Stearns

Author's Preface

My intent here is to resurrect the broad outlines of Palmerston's life and his world. This is not a biography in the strict sense of the word but a hybrid of textbook and biography that illustrates how one life interfaced with the world in a way that few have done in the past. A list of individuals who have left a major stamp on world culture would be short. Palmerston is one such individual but has been strangely overlooked. One reason perhaps is that in the last thirty years historians have moved away from political and diplomatic history and emphasized the history of social movements, cultural topics, and marginalized groups, such as the history of women, and racial and sexual minorities, to name a few. All this is good to the extent that historians can talk about and explore new areas that have too often been ignored. But to understand the spread of Western ideas and practice around the world in the last two centuries means we must understand how Britain, through free trade, tied together an international web of collaborating elites. The most crucial period in this development are found in the years between 1830 and 1870, during most of which period Lord Palmerston effectively managed foreign policy as foreign secretary and as prime minister. This book introduces the reader to Palmerston's life, his times, and his world. Since it is a text written without footnotes, a number of biographies and relevant sources are listed in the bibliographical essay in the back of the book.

Introduction

The question of British identity often hinges on what people think about the Victorian age, when Britain became a modern nation and then launched so much of the rest of the world into its modern form. In the twentieth century, Britain poured itself into a series of negative campaigns. The two world wars, the struggle against fascism and communism, and the drawn-out process of decolonization that unraveled an empire which had taken over three hundred years to construct did little to build a stable identity and a growing confidence. Certainly, modern citizens of the United Kingdom take pride in the peaceful image of their democracy and the achievements of their welfare state, but these rarely equate to the vehemence and energy of the negative ideals that have motivated the British elite in a series of campaigns that have left the citizens of modern Britain economically exhausted and bereft of a positive identity. Increasingly, politicians (and historians) scramble to define the meaning of the word "British," and struggle to understand the purpose of Britain in the postcolonial world. Should it be a part of Europe? Hold back from Europe? Serve as adjunct to the United States? Should Britain be proud or ashamed of its heritage as the progenitor of the Industrial Revolution? Does one proudly claim the imperial heritage that did so much (for better or worse) to modernize and globalize the world, or does one politely change the subject of conversation when the topic arises?

The founding of the Museum of Imperial and Commonwealth history, in Bristol, is a good example of this confusion over identity. That no museum of the British empire existed until quite recently speaks volumes about the way the British elite has handled the issue. When in the 1990s a small group of historians, politicians, and benefactors decided to open an institution that told the story of this vast global panorama, opposition arose from many quarters, particularly from the city counselors of Bristol. The museum directors decided to house their exhibits, tellingly, in the former railway terminus of the Great Western Railway, which had been designed by one of the great engineers of the Industrial revolution, Isambard Brunel. Bristol had long been a seaport that connected England to the world, and it played a substantial role in the slave trade. But why, the city counselors objected, should the citizens of Bristol establish a museum that threatened to glorify this shameful history and bring attention to an empire built by aristocrats and capitalists? Surely modern Britain is not about the projection of raw power but about diversity and tolerance. At that point the new project seemed politically dead. But then British citizens from India, Pakistan, Bangladesh, Africa, and the West Caribbean who lived in Bristol intervened. Wait a minute, they said, this is our history too. The empire is our past. We deserve a museum, and we deserve our story to be told. The project then moved forward and the museum, with no support from government bodies, came into being. One fact in this drama became unmistakably clear: British history in the nineteenth century is world history. Not all of it of course, but a great deal of it, and that also means that the history of Britain in the age of Palmerston is the history of many hundreds of millions of people from all over the globe.

The museum controversy is illustrative of conflicted feelings that historians bring to the study of the British past and, by derivation, to the Victorian period and to Palmerston. After the independence of most of the former colonies and territories in the 1950s and 1960s, much scholarship was nostalgic, wishing to trace the outlines of the imperial age, the narratives often tinged with sadness. While the age of Palmerston saw a series of conflicts around the world, burning like brushfires on the volatile edges of imperial expansion, it also saw the rise of Britain to an economic powerhouse, and, along with other centers in Europe, the nation enjoyed a cultural effusion of grace and confidence. This is a world that compares quite favorably to that of the twentieth century, with its mass murders and cultural misgivings. Some historians have regretted the loss of the Victorian world as the loss of civilization at its pinnacle, just as imagination takes many back to the glories of ancient democratic Athens or imperial Rome. Much of this scholarship focused on the political and constitutional understanding of empire.

New Imperialism in the last thirty years has battered away at this image, painting the imperial age of Britain as racist, sexist, and a brutal extension of power through military, cultural, and religious means, focusing mostly on the social history of Britain and its empire. It has also sought to show the "periphery" and the "metropole" as inexorably linked. Against New Imperialism new scholars have again returned to paint a triumphalist picture of Britain's role in the world, arguing, like Niall Ferguson, that Britain's place has been taken by its own progeny, the United States, and that, through the United States, Britain acting as elder statesman can still exert influence and play a beneficial role in the world.

No such self-doubt haunted the British public in the age of Palmerston. Certainly there was discord and conflict. Whether Chartists fighting for voting rights; aristocrats holding on to inherited wealth and political power; Methodist lay ministers preaching sanctification; gay people seeking company in "molly houses," pubs, or parks; or soldiers, sailors, or Irish migrants struggling to survive on low pay, none would have questioned the role of Britain in the world.

They all may have stressed different aspects of their identity as Anglicans or dissenters, workers, farmers, gentlemen, or Irish, Scottish, English, or Welsh. But they were British. They defined their own country and their own culture (and their own future) in optimistic and positive terms. They were perhaps, more or less, against absolutism on the continent, against what they saw as corrupt oriental despots, and against slavery. But they also believed in a great deal, and these positive ideals formed the characteristics of the mid-Victorian period: free trade, patriotism, parliamentary government, gentlemanly behavior, and of course, the excellence of their navy.

Palmerston played a remarkable role in this world. It was a period of time when the forces that remade Britain were in the process of remaking the world, and casting the world in a new mold—increasingly industrial, linked by global trade, mechanized, and then with rising elites, usually associated with the business class, forging new parliamentarian governments that were modeled on the British system. This book attempts to look at the life of Palmerston through the prism of high politics and social life, focusing foremost on Britain, and then on the world he influenced through empire and trade.

In his old age, the British public considered Lord Palmerston to be quintessentially British. His life and work represented in the imagination of millions of his countrymen the qualities of the country itself: energy and control, power and restraint, wealth, religion, military prowess (particularly on the sea), and tradition. Various components defined the idea of what it meant to be British: the English countryside, Protestantism, Parliament, the imperial city of London ruling over such places as Bengal, the Cape, innumerable islands in remote locations, and the white settlements of Canada, Australia, and New Zealand. Britain also meant the vanguard of progress that set the example of innovation in industry, of a balance between classes and wealth, of decent and restrained use of power that served as the arbiter of disputes around the world. As the nineteenth century historian John Seeley commented, trade and the empire of trade gave Britain its sparkle. What, he asked, would England be without its empire? And the British public in this period could very well have answered, and what would England be without Palmerston? Later generations have berated this period of history as one of hypocrisy and greed, dressed up in a dull and deadly cant. While this biography of Palmerston and his age cannot disagree with some of the criticism, it will be interesting to see how later generations compare the actions of our own elites on precisely these same issues.

1

Palmerston's England

This book traces the life of Henry John Temple and the world that he influenced. Historians refer to Henry John Temple, who lived from 1784 to 1865, by his aristocratic title, Lord Palmerston, referred to in this book simply as Palmerston. His fascinating career impacted the modern world to a greater extent than many more famous figures—yet few today know his name, or the fact that he served as Secretary of State for Foreign Affairs and then prime minister of Britain during most of the crucial years from 1830 until his death in 1865. This period saw Britain reach the zenith of its industrial power relative to the rest of the world. Palmerston influenced the world precisely because he guided British policy when Britain molded much of the modern world after its own image. Palmerston sought the prosperity of Britain through trade but also had far-reaching ambitions to change the nature of Britain's trading partners—in Lord Canning's famous phrase, to "make them English." He combined force, diplomacy, and trade to create a large informal empire of influence that paralleled and even surpassed the influence of Britain's growing formal empire. Latin America, the Middle East, Africa, India, and the Far East all faced momentous change due to the interventions of Palmerston. At his death in 1865 much of the modern world had been cast into the mold that Palmerston advocated—a world where constitutional government commanded the greatest respect, where free trade defined the economic relationship between countries, and where a new business and professional elite acted like a solvent against traditional culture and economic life and helped usher in the globalized world that we understand today.

Palmerston's career unfolded at home while Britain's prosperous economy steamed forward. As the first industrial nation of the world, Britain sat in the central hub of world trade. Britain earned its good luck, however with victory in war and prosperity at home. After the Napoleonic wars ended in 1815, Europeans wearily turned from the theater of conflict, and sought peace and stability. Although there were some wars, there were no continent-wide wars during this remarkable period for almost a hundred years, until WWI—historians call it the "long nineteenth century" for this reason. Taking advantage of the stability at home and peace in Europe, Britain extended its influence outward through trade and culture till its power, like waves rippling across a lake, lapped on the shore of every continent. The formal empire grew into the largest the world had ever known. It resulted from direct conquest, and in some cases inheritance—gaining pieces of empire from other European powers, usually part of peace negotiations, as when Britain gained islands in the Caribbean at the conclusion of the Napoleonic war. Britain also gained great influence in a process called "informal empire," where influence reached such a critical mass that it equated to imperialism.

Many scholars think Britain held an informal empire in parts of West Africa, the Middle East, the Far East, and the former Spanish colonies that gained independence in the 1820s. While land powers extended their territories—Russia extending its control east and south, and the United States pushing west into the American frontier—Britain, a sea power, reached overseas through trade and settlement into Africa, India, Australia, New Zealand, and a wide array of small places that seemed very remote and out of the way to British citizens. But even if many of the British did not fully comprehend the complexity of their empire, they expressed pride in their growing wealth, their cultural sophistication, and their status as a new Rome. James Thompson's famous poem, *Britannia*, though written in the eighteenth century, appealed strongly to Victorian sentiments on their "well-earned" empire guarded by her world-girdling trade and massive fleet.

But the empire in the nineteenth century differed much from the eighteenth-century version. In the early modern period, buccaneering European nations, beginning with Portugal, then Spain, the Netherlands, France, and Britain, built their overseas empires by force. No one in Europe imagined they needed an excuse to build empire—they conquered land to gain wealth and power and, sometimes, to spread Christianity. Europeans ruled because they could. The lust for power they considered a universal human trait, and it needed no excuse. In the Portuguese and Spanish empires, usually called "mixed" empires, the Europeans married and interbred with the indigenous inhabitants, creating new peoples such as the mestizos in the Spanish possessions in Latin America. In other areas the Portuguese intermarried and blended with the indigenous population, as in parts of the west coast of Africa. The French, British, and Dutch often took a different approach and built settler empires. In North America the British and the French settled along the eastern seaboard and built their new homes to look like the homes they had left behind. The Dutch in the Cape of Africa and British settlers in New Zealand and Australia turned these temperate regions into ethnic and cultural extensions of the home country. The conquered territory supplied raw material to the mother country and then bought, exclusively, manufactured goods in return. Economists called this a "mercantilist" empire because it operated on the theory that the home country should accumulate bullion and that the empire should trade exclusively within its own borders.

The mercantilist theory lost popularity with the loss of the American colonies and made the British rethink the colonial strategy. What first seemed a catastrophe soon taught an important lesson—without formal control, the British still maintained trade with the former colony and thus gained the benefit of the economic relationship without the military cost of holding it or defending its borders. The British in the early nineteenth century held a large quiltwork of formal colonies for purposes of trade. With the advent of industrialization, Britain realized it did not always need to shoulder the cost of colonies to engage in trade. Free trade protected her merchants from robbery or persecution where treaties with local governments enforced the rule of law and allowed British merchants to buy and to sell.

Force guaranteed free trade. After the Napoleonic war the British maintained a small army but had the largest navy in the world—larger than the next four naval powers combined. Even if all the naval powers of the world had opposed the British, the British could have at any time in the nineteenth century cleared the seas of enemy ships. This gave the British a powerful reach and the option to blockade, bombard from the sea, level coastal forts, and even to topple opposition far inland by sailing up rivers and bays. On a small scale the British fought constant wars. Skirmishes, while often major wars with the opponents of British imperialism, raged like brushfire at the fringes and served to expand the frontiers of the formal empire.

The wealthiest and most valued part of the empire—later called the dominions—required little defense, and they gained self-governance during the nineteenth century. This meant that first in Canada, then in Australia, New Zealand, and the Cape (now South Africa), a parliament and a cabinet with a prime minister answered to a governor appointed by Britain. The governor acted more as a constitutional monarch, and local citizens had control over their own internal affairs. White settlers primarily populated the dominions. They served the empire loyally, and the British government considered them capable of self-governance.

Most Britons considered British India to be the jewel in the crown of colonies. India gave Britain a powerful presence in Asia and a large trading partner. And India, self-sufficient, paid for itself. But most importantly India, as an ancient and exotic culture, fired the imagination of Victorians. Though the British empire sprawled over the whole world, most Victorians thought first of India when they thought of "the empire" outside of the dominions. At the time Palmerston held high office, Britain controlled most of India. But well into the middle of the nineteenth century, Britain still expanded her control of the subcontinent, particularly in the northwest. While India was the most prestigious part of the empire, the British never permanently settled it, ruling 200 to 300 million Indians in the Victorian era with not more than two hundred thousand people—this includes the British members of the Indian Civil Service, British soldiers, and British civilians. In 1857 the "Indian Mutiny" almost succeeded in loosening the British grip on the region, but British soldiers and loyal Indians put a damper on the revolt and finally defeated the rebels in their last holdouts. Overall, the Indians cooperated with British rule and most Indians, until the early part of the twentieth century, welcomed their presence. Even Gandhi, for instance, wrote that the British empire benefited its citizens, a position he held until the Amritsar Massacre of 1919, when British soldiers fired on a crowd of civilians. To be sure, resistance to British rule existed in most parts of the empire, but not to the extent that the leviathan of imperialism could be defeated. Many, like Henry Parnell, an Anglo-Irish politician, expressed opposition to the empire as early as 1830: "There are only three ways that the colonies can be of any advantage, 1. In furnishing a military force; 2. In supplying the parent state with a revenue, 3. In affording commercial advantages." He categorically denied that any of these three advantages accrued to the British by holding empire. But his opinion did not represent either the majority of the population, or what counted more, the elite. Questions did abound among many reformers, like Richard Cobden and John Bright, regarding the utility of the empire. More typical was the opinion of Bishop J. M. Thoburn, who spent his lifetime as a missionary in India during the time when Palmerston held office. He wrote that Britain held the reigns of empire because of a moral imperative.

> No living statesman, knowing the circumstances, would take it upon himself to withdraw the authority which now holds the vast Indian Empire in the embrace of peace, and let loose from the four winds all the elements of discord and rivalry, of ambition and avarice, of war and rapine, which must inevitably follow the departure of the last English ruler from the shores of India.

Empire depended as much on confidence, what some British observers called an "empire of opinion," as on force. Good opinion and prestige went hand in hand. Despite the sacrifices Britain made to attain victory over Napoleon, the victorious war effort went a long way to restore the prestige of Britain and console the public for the loss of the American colonies. In fact, Britain gained many more colonies by the end of the war. Britain gained Mauritius, the Cape of Good Hope, various islands in the West Indies, and Malta in the Mediterranean. In Europe, Britain took no advantage of its position as victor to gain territory, instead using its considerable influence at the Congress of Vienna to settle postwar issues equitably.

The Napoleonic Wars had cost a large sum of money—the government raised huge loans as bonds that came due at interest. It also cost Britain in blood—over two hundred thousand men in uniform had died. Moreover the war led to a social and political backlash against republican ideals. The radical nature of the French Revolution led to a backlash against radical egalitarian ideas in Britain among both the evangelical middle class and the landed elite. Parliament passed the Combination Acts of 1799–1800, which prohibited workers from "combining" to force wages higher. In 1813–14, Parliament repealed the medieval regulation of wages that did much to protect workers.

The Industrial Revolution

The Industrial Revolution inflated British power. This revolution did not happen overnight but sprang from a number of other slow-working changes in society.

Like a pair of horses, a demographic revolution accompanied an agricultural revolution. Historians describe this as a slow population explosion. The population rose incrementally from 1650 to 1750 and then picked up speed, increasing steadily from 1750 all through the nineteenth century. Ireland proved the exception: Ireland dropped in population between 1845 and 1848, when bacterial infection rotted out potato crops and mass starvation decimated the Irish populace. But demographic growth, though uneven, raised Britain from just over 5 million people in 1715 to just over 10 million in 1815. This occurred for a number of reasons, among them a burgeoning agricultural output. More food meant healthier people, people more resistant to disease, and people with lower infant mortality.

But increased standards of living also led to a larger population. The average age of marriage for a male dropped from twenty-eight to twenty-four. In a society with a very low out-of-wedlock birthrate, earlier marriage meant larger families. The increased productivity on agricultural land meant that without increasing the rural population food production would support the growing urban centers. In 1750, London had over seven hundred thousand people, but by 1801 the city would have over a million, by 1851 over 2 million, and by 1901 over 6 million. Larger cities meant crowded conditions, lack of sanitation, and growing slums. This in turn led many to nostalgia for life as it had been before the growth of large urban areas. Poet and novelist William Morris dreamed up a nonindustrial England in 1854 that was "small, and white, and clean," and free of "steam and piston stroke."

Increased population fueled the growing factories in the cities, emigration to the rapidly expanding empire overseas, and emigration to the United States and other areas of the world outside the formal empire. It also helped keep wages lower and break down traditional crafts and guilds that had dominated certain fields of labor. Other cities besides London experienced rapid growth—such as Birmingham, Leeds, Manchester, and Liverpool, among others.

The preconditions of the Industrial Revolution are easier to pinpoint than the cause. Population growth provided a steady stream of laborers to the urban centers where the factories hired them. Population growth and higher agricultural productivity also kept food and wage costs lower, and this in turn increased profit for factory owners. But other conditions contributed to the revolution.

In truth, England had produced iron, coal, and cotton garments long before the Industrial Revolution. The Celts produced iron before Rome conquered the southern part of Britain. Medieval guilds sold wool clothing to Europe. In the seventeenth century, manufacturers used waterwheels to run bellows and wood fuel to fire furnaces that produced iron. But with deforestation, the price of firewood rose. In addition, charcoal from the wood fuel produced impurities in the iron. Smiths working in their forges took this inferior iron, called pig iron, and hammered the red-hot metal on an anvil, pounding out the impurities. Then a new discovery enabled iron manufacturers to raise productivity and quality at the same time.

When manufacturers applied heat to coal, it burned off impurities and a quality charcoal remained, called coke. This enabled manufacturers to substitute coke for wood charcoal to produce a better product, and enabled the iron factories to locate near coal mines, not merely near local forests and streams. Fortunately, coal lay close to the surface and in many convenient locations. But even so, owners had to transport the coal, and this increased the demand for iron barges and for rails on which wagons hauled the coal. So the very success in manufacturing more iron also led to a demand for more iron, to say nothing of the export of iron weapons and cannonry around the world. Efficiency and quality in the production of iron guaranteed a ready market.

The increase in the quality and quantity of iron led to demands for more coal. A series of critical inventions resolved the bottlenecks that arose when one link in the chain of production outpaced other links. Coal owners profited from the demand for coal and not only opened new mines but dug deep into the ground—often right under the coastline and under the sea. Miners sometimes heard the surf off the coast of Wales rolling large boulders overhead on the floor of the sea. However these deep mines often filled with water, making it impossible to follow the seam of coal further. But the invention of steam pumps drained the water from the coal mines far more efficiently than human-or animal-drawn pumps. Steam engines also drew carts along rails by using rope or chains. The steam engines turned wheels like those on the Boulton and Watt steam engine that in the 1780s transformed a variety of industries such as weaving. Advances in one area led to increased productivity that only revealed a bottleneck in another area that technological innovation again resolved.

This improved mechanization multiplied the effects of human labor and revolutionized the production of textiles. The growing population in Britain had a tremendous appetite for clothing, and the overseas empire only added to the immense dimensions of this potential market. Textiles had been made by hand, in "weavers cottages" on handlooms and spinning wheels. A series of inventions increased productivity: James Hargreaves' Spinning Jenny, Richard Arkwright's Water Frame, and then further improvements with Samuel Crompton's Spinning Mule, and Edmund Cartwright's Power Loom. These inventions, fed by the importation of cotton and wool from overseas, allowed factories to produce massive quantities of textiles cheaply. Much of the world, not just the British empire, devoured the high-quality and cheaply priced textiles.

Many other areas of the world besides Britain possessed similar preconditions, but no Industrial Revolution occurred in those places. Ireland had increased population but did not initiate the Industrial Revolution. Germany and France had deposits of coal, iron, and dwindling supplies of forest. Holland actively traded throughout the world and shared in the advances of the seventeenth century, as did most of northwestern Europe. Why Britain? And why then? As Professor Heyck has pointed out, "The preconditions for industrialization and a set of people capable of exploiting them alike came to exist in eighteenth-century Britain but not elsewhere (at least to the same degree) and not before." He means by this that Britain possessed not only the material preconditions but also the social preconditions that made the Industrial Revolution possible.

The social conditions included a landed elite that won from the British crown the legal right of absolute property. Unlike landlords in Europe, the elite in Britain owned their land absolutely, including the mineral rights. They could buy and sell their land, and they tolerated very little interference from the government in the use of their property. Landlords made property safe, and the rule of law protected the acquisition of wealth. Add entrepreneurs to this mix of social preconditions. Enterprising businessmen fueled the Industrial Revolution, most of them "dissenters," members of Protestant sects outside of the established Anglican church: Methodists, Quakers, Baptists, Congregationalists, and Presbyterians, among others. After 1828, with the repeal of the Test and Corporations Act, dissenters could enroll but not take degrees from Oxford and Cambridge Universities. Before 1828, dissenters had to take advantage of an annual indemnity that allowed them to hold office. While after 1828 restrictions were lifted, many dissenters channeled much of their social energy into business, where they had no restrictions. They also possessed a strong desire for social advancement. They shared the values of the Protestant Reformation, which stressed ethics of hard work and thrift and independent thought. These dissenters, though a clear minority, nonetheless made up a good half of entrepreneurs and helped take advantage of the favorable conditions that lay behind the Industrial Revolution.

The revolution's explosion of wealth translated into not just trade but power. Britain became the first modern industrialized country in the world. As such, it was the most influential, for British influence spread not just through formal empire and a powerful navy but also through example—the desire of elites from around the world to emulate Britain and share in the expanse of wealth. Britain, without at first the conscious desire to do so, became a model of efficiency, wealth, and fashion, thus exporting not only manufactured goods to much of the world but also its civilization. That meant more than just business; it meant the exportation of culture—philosophy, literature, political ideas, modes of recreation, such as tea and cookies for a midmorning and midafternoon break, and sports like cricket, and of course, the English language, today the lingua franca of the world.

The Industrial Revolution was a process, not an event. The process involved higher levels of economic growth, moved manufacturing from domestic manufacture to factories, and radically increased the productivity of workers. For example, yarn began to be spun in factories instead of in homes. Only 750 employees in a cotton mill manufactured the same amount of yarn produced by two hundred thousand home-based yarn spinners. Between 1760 and 1830 the Industrial Revolution transformed Britain, creating a new economy of vast productivity and technological advancement that operated in concert with—not always against—the traditional economy. Wealth so radically increased that Great Britain became unquestionably the richest country on earth and, together with expanding trade, the single largest trading partner for most areas of the globe. While Britain had extensive trade with Europe, it tied together the largest economies of the world. That meant, for example, that India, China, Argentina, and the United States all traded more with Britain than with any other country. Britain sat in the middle of a global web of trade created by her own exploding economy.

The results of the Industrial Revolution changed the face of Britain and eventually of the whole world. Wages rose. But at first the increased wealth did not appear to benefit the workers. Slums in the cities, smoke, polluted water supplies, children working in factories, the erosion of traditional forms of crafts and the erosion of traditional gender roles, all these created social havoc in Britain. The landed elites who ran the British government benefited from the increased wealth, the trade, and the power that the Industrial Revolution gave to them and to their government. But social unrest haunted the elite, not least for fear of a French-like revolution that could sweep them from power. The reactions to the Industrial Revolution, and not just the Industrial Revolution itself, radically changed society. The Industrial Revolution created power for the British elite, provoked pride in progress and innovation, and also kindled the fear of upheaval.

A downside accompanied the industrial changes. When Queen Victoria came to the throne, one in eleven citizens eked out a hardscrabble living as paupers. The poor swarmed into Leeds, Manchester, Birmingham, and London, seeking work. The rising professional elite, from novelists to journalists to philosophers, wrote scandalized accounts about the horrific conditions. Developers packed row houses close together with little or no space for lawns or gardens. Large older houses that once held a single family with servants housed up to eight people in a room. Whole districts consisted of unlit streets filled with rotting slums, partially collapsed roofs, and multilevel porches spanning open sewage ditches. These often unpoliced districts festered with social ills—airless rooms where families slept together on rags, children swarming through the dark narrow alleyways, skinny from malnutrition, half-clothed, and often sick. The countryside reflected these conditions like a dirty mirror, with small cottages that went unrepaired for generations, open ditches for sewage, wages so low that the poor agricultural workers wore threadbare clothing. Worse, the underfed poor suffered from taxation on food, with the Corn Laws taxing grains and tariffs on meat, peas, and a wide variety of staples. The government also taxed soap and windows, making cleanliness, and even light itself, difficult for the poor to attain.

The push to reform society and governmental policy was accompanied by an astounding pace of technical improvement. Transportation technology is one example. Traveling by coach had been much improved in the latter eighteenth century by the process of "macadamizing" roads, leveling them off and pressing gravel into the earth until the road presented a level and hard surface. Canals in the late eighteenth century crisscrossed much of Britain, enabling the cheap transportation of coal and other heavy or bulky commodities. Palmerston grew up with these achievements, but he saw in his lifetime the birth of the railway and its extension across Britain and much of the world. James Watt, a Scottish engineer, made the use of steam practical with his inventions. But another Englishman, George Stephenson, took steam technology, improved it, and used the power of steam to pull a train along fixed rails.

Many members of Parliament, in granting legal authority to build railway lines across private property, doubted that roads could remain level across swamps without sinking under the weight of the trains. One prominent observer in Liverpool, who afterward became inspector of Post-office trains, declared flatly that steam engines could never travel faster than ten miles an hour, and if proved wrong, he would eat a stewed engine wheel for breakfast. Despite such doubts, trains whisked the first railway passengers along in 1825 on the Stockton and Darlington railroad line. Under Stephenson's direction a railway linked the large and growing industrial town of Manchester with the port city of Liverpool. The train, named the "Rocket," built in 1829, caused a sensation throughout the newspaper-reading world and showed its power to reimagine distance and time by racing along at twenty miles an hour—a phenomenal speed for the age. The trains quickly changed the face of Britain, connecting the major cities in a web of steel that magnified its economic power and made Britain a model of modernity for Europe, the United States, and the world.

Corn Laws

After the collapse of Napoleon's embargo on trade with Britain, known as the "Continental System," cheap grain flooded the market from Germany and elsewhere. British farmers suffered terribly from the precipitous fall in prices. Parliament responded by passing the "Corn Laws" in 1815. The Corn Laws attempted to remedy the flood of cheap wheat by forbidding the importation of wheat until domestic prices reached 80s a quarter, or approximately $2.50 a bushel. While this admirably protected farmers, it also raised the price of bread significantly and kept food prices high by heavily taxing incoming food items, and acted as a subsidy to support a largely anti-reform minded landed elite. The Corn Laws became a defining point of conflict between classes for the next few decades.

As Britain transformed itself from an agricultural country to an industrial country, the battle over the Corn Laws reflected the societal strains of this transition. Britain exported manufactured goods but imported agricultural products. Part of the transition necessitated the psychological adjustment of the elite because the farms of Britain no longer fed a self-sufficient British people. The "hungry forties" exasperated the conflict over the Corn Laws. Unemployment ran high and many working-class families lacked enough food for proper nutrition.

These conditions partly explain the controversy that surrounded the Corn Laws and, later, the Anti–Corn Law League. Food taxation vitally affected the well-being of the poor. But also, the suffering of the poor inspired many humanitarians to promote free trade as progressive, avant-garde, and humane.

Free trade appeared to solve the problem of poverty on a number of fronts. First, it stimulated trade, thus jobs. Free trade meant the abolition of the Corn Laws, and this lowered the price of food for the poor. Today many label the advocates of free trade as "right wing." At that time, conservatives labeled the advocates of free trade as radicals and idealists.

Mill owners centered in the manufacturing north of England, particularly around Manchester, led the fight against the Corn Laws. Their fight for tax reform did not entail support for all issues of reform, however. Richard Cobden, for instance, the principal spokesman for the movement, opposed limiting the hours of workmen and opposed any form of government meddling in the factories. He argued that if workers did not like their conditions, they could always emigrate to another country. Cobden did not support the Chartist movement that sought universal suffrage for all men over the age of twenty-one. He battled for the interests of the manufacturers and predicted that free trade would remake England and, he hoped, the world, in the middle-class mold. Though wealthy, he saw himself as a representative of the middle class, and his movement as a middle-class movement. He wrote, "We have carried it on by those means which the middle class usually carries on its movements. We have had our meetings of dissenting ministers; we have obtained the co-operation of the ladies; we have resorted to tea-parties, and taken those pacific means for carrying out our view which mark us rather as a middle-class set of agitators."

He also dreamed of remaking the world by free trade into the English mold. In his pamphlet on England, Ireland, and America he writes of his dream for an exciting new future using the moribund Ottoman empire as an example. He wrote,

> Constantinople, outrivaling New York, may be painted, with a million of free citizens, as the focus of all the trade of Eastern Europe. Let us conjure up the thousands of miles of railroads, carrying to the very extremities of this empire—not the sanguinary satrap, but the merchandise and the busy traders of a free state; conveying—not the Firman of a ferocious Sultan, armed with death to the trembling slave, but the millions of newspapers and letters which stimulate the enterprise and excite the patriotism of an enlightened people. Let us imagine the Bosporus and the Sea of Marmora swarming with steamboats, connecting the European and Asiatic continents by hourly departures and arrivals; or issuing from the Dardanelles, to reanimate once more with life and fertility the hundred islands of the Archipelago; or cover the rich shores of the Black Sea in the power of the New Englander, and the Danube pouring down its produce on the plains of Moldavia and Walachia, now subject to the plough of the hardy Kentuckian. Let us picture the Carolinians, the Virginians, and the Georgians transplanted to the coasts of Asia Minor, and behold its hundreds of cities again bursting from the tomb of ages, to recall religion and civilization to the spot from whence they first issued forth up on the world.

In the fall of 1842, Cobden met a young Quaker who earned his living spinning cotton in a small house in Leamington, England. The young man brooded over the death of his young wife. Cobden, who knew the young man as a friend, comforted him with words that the young man John Bright claimed changed his life, and through him, changed the history of the country. Cobden said, "There are thousands of houses in England at this moment where wives, mothers and children are dying of hunger," he said. "Now, when the first paroxysm of your grief is past, come with me, and we will never rest till the Corn Law is repealed."

John Bright, channeling his sorrow into productive activism, crusaded across Britain to eliminate the Corn Laws, arguing that they propped up a corrupt, unproductive landed elite, and taxed the food of the poor, creating shortages and exacerbating poverty among the lower classes. Even many landlords saw the necessity of eliminating the Corn Laws. When the Conservative prime minister Robert Peel proposed to reform the laws in the early 1840s, he understood that the good intent behind the Corn Laws had created unseen hardships. For instance, when the price of wheat rose, then the tax on wheat fell. In theory this meant that when the imported price of these food items rose the tax fell, and when the price fell to a certain point, the tax spiked higher, keeping equilibrium of prices for the farmer and the consumer. But in fact, as Peel pointed out, suppliers of wheat and other products hoarded their supply until the price rose and only then sold the goods, thus keeping the cost of food high and creating an artificial scarcity.

Backed by large donations from rich manufacturers Cobden, Bright, and the new rising middle classes of Britain pushed for the total abolition of the Corn Laws. They formed the National Anti–Corn Law League, which, between 1838 and 1846, sponsored thousands of meetings with roving lecturers and agitators handing out literature and giving speeches in every district of Britain, taking the anti–corn law propaganda into the heartland of the Tory countryside. A final tragedy doomed the Corn Laws. In 1845 the potato crop failed in Ireland, causing massive starvation. It seemed untenable to keep a tax on imported food when so many starved. Under the administration of Peel, a liberal Tory who Palmerston greatly admired, Parliament abolished the notorious Corn Laws. The bill passed with a minority of Conservative party support, and Peel had to rely heavily on the Whigs. While prosperity returned in the later 1840s, the issue of protection did not completely go away until around 1860. Because of this independence, for many years, until the 1860s, the "Peelites" stood out as a group divided from the mainstream Conservative and Whig parties.

Free Trade

While the issues of free trade divided classes in Britain, the edges blur on close inspection. The rising urban and middle classes inclined toward business, the landed elite to a patrician and rural economy. But the British landed elite differed radically from the landed elite on the continent, which tended to eschew involvement in business affairs. In Europe the large landowners left their estates in the care of bailiffs and congregated heavily in salons, attended extravagant dances, ate epicurean delights at gold-laced dining tables in Paris, Versailles, Vienna, Madrid, and St. Petersburg, usually while fawning on the ruling monarch. But the British landed elite—while sharing a need to constantly socialize—had distinct differences.

The British monarchs under the Hanoverian kings George III and IV, and then Queen Victoria, did not glitter like the European courts—the British monarchy kept most events practical and unpretentious, with more interest in an evening of backgammon and whist than in the minuet and sumptuous feasts. The monarchy reflected an English gentleman's household writ large, with questions of farming, marriage, appointments, and parliamentary gossip the most likely topics of conversation. The British monarchy had ritual, wealth, and real power but tended to show it off less and exercise its power with more caution.

The practical bent of the British manifested itself from the monarchy, the landed elite, and all the way down to agricultural laborers. This may explain the peculiarly British dedication to free trade—because all levels of society involved themselves in business and profited from it. The commitment of the landed elite to free trade marked them off from their elite cousins on the continent and perhaps goes a long way to explain the British development of industry before any other region on earth.

As has already been remarked, middle-class dissenters played a large role in entrepreneurial activity. But the landed elite participated in key ways that provided leadership, resources, and funding for larger business enterprises to take root; they were what Professors Anthony Hopkins and Peter Cain call "gentlemanly capitalists." Canals for navigation, preceding the railway as a network of transport from one region to another, necessarily crossed land owned by the large landowners. The Duke of Bridgewater, for instance, pioneered the construction of canals for barge transport. By 1906, the Royal Commission of Canals reported a total of thirty-nine hundred miles of canals, all built by a remarkable combination of aristocratic land, finance, and middle-class genius and organization. Railways showed a similar cooperation and return on profit, whose success fired the imagination of the public as well as providing great convenience and wealth.

From the 1840s on, when popular turmoil came to a full boil with the Chartist movement for parliamentary reform, the economic depression, and agitation to end the Corn Laws—things suddenly began to get better. Britain embarked, as the eminent Professor G. M. Trevelyan wrote, to "the simultaneous rapid increase of steam traffic, British trade—stagnant since 1815 and moribund in 1842—began to go forward on its amazing journey of Victorian prosperity." The Industrial Revolution held out great promise, as did free trade, but this became overwhelmingly apparent only in the 1840s. With the lowering of taxes the masses could afford cheap imports, industry began to grow and the wages of the laboring poor went up. The business class made more money than ever, and even the landed elite, losing power in relative terms, found new prosperity in agriculture, investments, and the minerals buried in their land. When Tory leader Robert Peel proposed the abolition of the Corn Laws he marked a new epoch in British history—the end of the old right and the birth of the new right. While the Tory party did not give up on the Corn Laws until 1852, its members increasingly came to share the laissez-faire economics of the Whigs, and later the Liberals. This meant that Britain, until the rise of the labor party after World War I, had two major parties dedicated to the doctrine of free trade. From this point on, few seriously challenged free trade in Britain until the 1930s. The primacy of this doctrine, coupled with the British empire, formal and informal, ignited the process of globalization in most regions of the world.

One of the harder influences to trace on the Victorian mind during Palmerston's life is the influence of philosophical ideas. Economist Adam Smith formulated many of the current ideas about the benefits of free trade. But many other prominent thinkers shared similar ideas. Emmanuel Kant, the German philosopher, predicted in the late eighteenth century that men, through the natural desire to protect their private property, would unfold a "hidden plan" by providence to advance civilization through free trade, and that this would lead to peace between the great European powers that would eventually expand to the entire world. War simply would not be worth the lost profit, and a "lawful federation" of nations would emerge. This optimism, whether traceable to Kant or not, animated the public mind of Britain from the 1840s to World War I.

Reform

The first half of the nineteenth century has been called "the age of reform" because reform acts reordered much of society and made it compatible with a new industrial age. The Repeal of the Test and Corporations Acts of 1828, the Catholic Emancipation Act of 1829, the Great Reform Act of 1832, the Factory Act of 1833, the Poor Law Amendment Act of 1834, the Prison Act of 1835, the Municipal Corporations Act of 1835, the Committee on Education in 1839, the Lunacy Act of 1845, and the Public Health Act of 1845, passed Parliament in rapid fire, a flurry of initiatives that reformed society forever well before Palmerston became prime minister.

Jeremy Bentham and his doctrine of Utilitarianism may have influenced many lawmakers who passed legislation that reformed British society in the mid-Victorian period. Bentham's ideas fit nicely with the rising middle class, and also harmonized with the new social conditions created by increased urbanization and the rise of an industrial society. New industrial regulations, church reform, metropolitan improvements, changes in the divorce law, and reform of the criminal code all fit neatly with Bentham's ideas of reform, which can be summed up as "the greatest good for the greatest number." Bentham argued that "every action should be judged right or wrong according to how far it tends to promote or damage the happiness of the community." This very practical approach to social problems appealed to the Victorian mind and provided intellectual grist and vigor to the rhetoric of reform. This approach also kindled fiery attacks against reform by conservatives claiming that utilitarianism pulled Britain downward toward a mechanical, bureaucratic, and dehumanizing modern society, far removed from "jolly England."

The Poor Law Amendment Act of 1834 offers a good example of the reformist impulse. It attempted to bring "the greatest good to the greatest number" yet it magnified the suffering of the poor. Previously each parish in Britain gave help to the indigent as needed, often with cash payments that allowed the unemployed worker, widow, or disabled enough to live on. They still lived with their own families or by themselves in small quarters, usually a slum dwelling in the city or a cottage in rural areas. But the new reform law required parishes to unite into larger more efficient "unions" and then create workhouses that were so unpleasant that the unemployed would be sure to avoid them and seek gainful employment. The Poor Law's workhouses separated the sexes and channeled all work on the poorhouse site for close supervision, making the recipients of aid feel like prisoners, penned in and watched. While the Poor Laws did provide much needed help, it made the poor miserable, and most resented the workhouses.

Other legislation cut against the inclinations of business owners who resented the imposition of a ten-hour workday, first for children and then later for adults. This seemed to interfere with property rights and to inject centralized government over local tradition and authority. By the 1850s, the size of the British state had grown considerably, though it was still small by continental standards. New laws regulated many levels of society. This meant roving inspectors, listening to the testimony and oversight of "experts," which in turn meant a growth of and enrichment of a professional class whose licensed labor gave them incomes far above what market rates would have paid them. Thus many intellectual historians credit Bentham for needed reforms, while others blame him for the start of the welfare state and even the beginnings of authoritarian governmental policies.

Class and Society

Nineteenth-century society made fine distinctions of class. While many in Palmerston's society stressed the importance of pedigree, most stressed the importance of money. After the revolution of 1688 in which landlords won absolute control over their own property, money purchased class standing. Family ties still defined social precedence, but in the century preceding Palmerston's birth, and certainly during his life, Britain had an open elite. Wealth purchased land, which in turn defined upper-class status. Society at the very top included around three hundred families, most of whom owned over ten thousand acres of land and derived their income from renting to tenant farmers. Still upper crust, but one step lower, was the gentry. They constituted around three thousand families owning anywhere from a thousand to ten thousand acres of land. Those below these upper-class squires formed the middle class, what we would today call the upper middle class. They constituted around 15 percent of the population at the birth of Palmerston, and then around 20 percent of the population in the 1850s and 60s, at the height of his career—clearly a growing force in early and mid-Victorian society. Beneath the middle class, scratching out a precarious living, labored the working class. Each class—the landed, middle, and working class—divided into conflicting camps. But they each shared a common consciousness of their place in a vertically stratified society.

The upper class changed greatly as Palmerston grew up. Before the French Revolution, in the eighteenth century, the landed elite ruled as a paternalistic class—the country squire headed local government and ran the national government as members of Parliament or the House of Lords, with younger sons filling the ranks of officers in the army and navy. Younger sons also had careers open to them in the professions as clergy in the church, lawyers at the bar, or as medical doctors. The landlord often appointed the clergy in the village that lay on his property, mediated conflict as justice of the peace and, at his best, provided not only employment on his estate but medicine for sick tenants and agricultural workers and provided emergency food for families down on their luck.

The French Revolution and the Industrial Revolution acted as an acid that began to dissolve the hierarchical structure of society, where each order understood its place and looked upward with deference to the leadership of its betters. Landlords increasingly agreed with the new liberalism that turned society from patronage and privilege to one of contract. With enclosure the open land system changed to large agri-business enterprises, sending superfluous workers to the city as factory workers and turning those who remained into agricultural laborers working for the landlord on a salary. With the investment opportunities created by a ready market for minerals on estates and the profit made by canals and then railways, landlords turned aside from the traditions that ordered agricultural society. Thomas Carlyle, the prominent nineteenth-century literary figure, dubbed this the "abdication of the governors."

The rising middle class created many of the changes that transformed society from one of tradition to contract. As a business and professional class, the middle class made its money in an industrial economy that rapidly expanded as Palmerston came of age. Because the middle class made its money from business, they clamored for free trade and defended the protection of property from governmental interference and excessive taxes. They also strongly advocated reform that broadened the definition of who could vote and forced Parliament to jettison the "rotten boroughs" where local landowners virtually appointed representatives.

Dissenters made up at least half of the middle class and they were strongly evangelical. The middle class frowned on many of the values of the landed class—they often disliked hunting, theater, dancing, and recreation such as cock fighting and horse racing, as a waste of time, and particularly disapproved of these activities on Sundays. The middle class set the moral tone for Britain, a tone that the upper class absorbed and then soon represented. Even Queen Victoria expressed herself in a moral style that reflected the sense of self-control, discipline, prudery, and conscience of the middle class. From the middle class also flowed the passion for reform stemming from the evangelical impulse to view life as a spiritual journey. John Wesley, the founder of Methodism, preached the doctrine of "Christian Perfection," which asserted that with love filling the human heart, sin could be rooted out entirely from one's life. Though most dissenters did not go so far as this, they did believe in reforming themselves and society. From evangelicals came a powerful motivation to improve themselves, society, and the world, from sanitation, police, sewers, and forest preservation to the abolition of slavery.

While the middle class had the power to effect most of these changes, the working class, far less influential, made up almost 80 percent of the population of Britain. Its members labored in fields, factories, and artisan shops and served as plumbers and machinists. "Navvies" built the railroads and dug tunnels in gangs. The working class mined for coal and macadamized the roads, laying down the rock and gravel that turned a mud field into a paved road serviceable year-round. The working class included the sailors and soldiers that guarded and expanded the empire, as well as the domestic servants who worked for not only the landed elite but the middle class as well. By the time Palmerston took office for the first time workers and the middle class had begun to identify horizontally instead of vertically. They did not look above and below to define themselves but looked around. Some scholars argue that the Industrial Revolution created class-consciousness because during this time workers and the middle class gained awareness of themselves.

With working-class awareness came increased conflict as workers began to drop deference to their social superiors and to voice their grievances to the ruling elite. Riots and political assemblages, not unheard of in the eighteenth century, increased up through the 1840s as the Industrial Revolution wreaked havoc on traditional society. The Peterloo Massacre, in 1819, is one such example, where demonstrators gathered to voice support for repeal of the Corn Laws and for parliamentary reform. Volunteer militia, drawn largely from the middle class, charged the crowd and killed eleven people and wounded hundreds more. With the example of the French Revolution ever in mind, the ruling class at this time came to fear the prospect of a British Revolution. Even the most prominent political leaders at times felt afraid for their lives and the lives of their families. Robert Peel, then prime minister, wrote from London to his wife on their country estate, "May God preserve you and watch over you and my children. I have requested some new arms in perfect order and ammunition to be sent to Drayton. . . . I think one of the rooms in the Tower would be the safest place of deposit." She fearlessly replied, "During the whole of this late tumultuous scene . . . our arrangements were quietly and vigorously made and should have been equal to an attack from two or three hundred till assistance came. . . . I am confident that no men actually attacking doors and windows here would have left this place alive." The landed classes were fearful but also highly reactive.

Science, Secularization, and Religion

While secularism seeped into the fabric of life after the 1850s, the bold pattern of religion by no means disappeared. Throughout the first part of the nineteenth century, Britain became increasingly religious. Most Britons still practiced their faith, and very few disavowed Christian beliefs openly. Rather, as urbanization increased, church attendance declined substantially for the working class, even as evangelical fervor slowly increased its sway. But a counter trend was also apparent: among the highly literate the advances of naturalistic science had begun to erode confidence in the literal truth of the scriptures.

Secularization had been growing slowly in Britain, as in Europe, for a few hundred years. The Protestant Reformation itself exhibited secular tendencies for promoting a simplified and rationalized Christian faith and eradicating many of the popular beliefs prominent in the Middle Ages that provided a pantheon of saints with special powers of intervention and help. The Enlightenment further eroded belief in Christian doctrine. Philosophers in the eighteenth century questioned revelation as a source of truth and claimed to appeal only to the bar of reason and evidence for their conclusions. Religion, to philosophers like Voltaire and Rousseau, preached superstition. Rationalists would reorder society and govern not by immutable laws laid down by clergy or the pope in Rome but by thinking citizens.

The clergy of the Church of England in the eighteenth century had adopted many of the ideas of the Enlightenment and leaned toward rationalism. They often gave polished and philosophical sermons that lacked warmth and religious devotion. The evangelical revival in the latter part of the eighteenth century and in the first part of the nineteenth century challenged the coldness of the Church of England. Methodism, founded by the Anglican priest John Wesley, preached a religion of the heart and a devotion to Christian perfection. His "holiness movement" influenced other denominations as well, even the Church of England, until the tone of Victorian society reflected the ethics of the evangelicals—a desire for personal spiritual improvement, and an impulse to reach out and help others in need.

The evangelicals did not form a particular denomination, but constituted a type of religious personality found in the Church of England (where most resided) or any number of other Protestant denominations. They inherited the Puritan tradition with some key differences. They shared with the Puritans a serious and devotional approach to their faith and a belief that Christian teachings inform all areas of life. Unlike the Puritans, evangelicals tended to believe, for the most part, in free will. They advocated conversion to Christ and crusaded against drinking, gambling, and sexual immorality. Their base of support in the middle class and their distinctly entrepreneurial tendencies led most of them to side politically with the Whigs. But for the most part they rejected the radical wing of the Whig party. The radicals absorbed and advocated the ideas of the French Revolution. This included the rationalism of the enlightenment and the implied rebellion against authority and the disturbing specter of atheism. The evangelicals opposed Catholicism and the "high church" liturgical movement in the Church of England called the Oxford movement, started by John Henry Newman, that traced the Church of England from Roman Catholic roots. They demanded from themselves and their peers a high standard of personal conduct. Since many owned large estates and sat both in Parliament and the House of Lords, they swayed the aristocracy in Britain to moderate their pleasures, particularly their love of drinking and gambling, as an example for the growing numbers of working class in the cities.

Evangelicals influenced not only the cultural tone of Victorian society as a whole—from the queen to the factory worker—but also politics. Their beliefs introduced new approaches to political issues that still prevail in world affairs today. The evangelicals demanded reform not only from individuals but also from society. Evangelical influence percolated among the middle class and began to seep upward to the aristocracy. The "Clapham Saints," led by the great antislavery crusader William Wilberforce, inculcated evangelical values in the landed elite. He purposely campaigned to reform the aristocracy and argued that if the elite set the proper example the working-class men and women would follow.

This latter impulse lay behind the drive for reform, and worked to improve society until Christians rooted out the last vestiges of inefficiency and injustice. Not only the antislavery movement but suffrage, even early environmentalism, owed much to this movement's impulse to change the world. Its proponents ushered in a new philosophy of governance that critiqued governmental actions. They insisted that governments operate more openly according to a discernable and agreed upon law of nations that answered to a Christian conscience. As such, governments should launch wars reluctantly, wield force sparingly, and then solely in self-defense or for a higher cause. Nations should build empires only for the good of those ruled. Governments should practice morality no less than the Christian individuals who make up a Christian citizenry. Outspoken and organized, evangelicals, though few in number, cast a long shadow.

But other forces worked against this revival of faith. When agricultural workers began leaving the countryside and working in the cities, they often left their religious ties at home. The Church of England responded by building too few new churches for the working poor. Many of these workers stayed home from church on Sunday too tired from the exhausting workweek to get up early and attend a religious service. They preferred going to the local pubs, or watching local sports games, cockfighting, or boxing matches. The evangelicals roused themselves against this trend by recruiting and building churches in the growing cities, but not fast enough to stop the slide of church attendance.

The march of science among the highly literate gave secularism another push. Charles Lyell's book *Principles of Geology* argued for the immense age of the Earth, a genealogy that far exceeded the ten to twelve thousand years postulated by conservative clergy. Charles Darwin published his groundbreaking *On the Origin of Species* in 1859. In this work Darwin presented evidence gathered during his trip on the H.M.S. *Beagle* in Latin America, particularly the

Galápagos Islands, that species competed to survive, and this competition led to the dominance of certain traits—changes that added up to the evolution of one species from another. In literature, a scientific and rationalistic approach to the Bible itself greatly damaged faith in the literal truth of the Bible. German criticism—so called because German academics pioneered this rational approach to scripture—discovered contradictions in the Bible and tried to separate religious myth from historical truth. These developments, while damaging, were not always incompatible with faith, and many religious thinkers attempted to forge a synthesis between science and religion.

In the Church of England the Oxford movement led by John Henry Newman attempted to place Christian theology on an aesthetic and subjectivist foundation. Newman emphasized the liturgy and ritual of the medieval church. He argued for changes in the church service that raised the bar of aesthetic taste very high, and this did appeal to many who found increased devotion through art and symbolism. Conservative Christians also began in the Victorian era to pull away from science and challenge the increasing worldliness of society. Many Christians in both the Church of England and dissenting churches emphasized the societal improvements that application of the gospel would bring.

Gender Roles

Religion, particularly evangelical Christianity reinforced traditional gender roles. Jane Austin's novel *Pride and Prejudice* gives a true-to-life picture of upper-class women and their role in society in this period. The education of a girl prepared her for marriage. Aristocratic young women searched for a suitable husband as their main business in life. Girls from the upper class sometimes, though not always, attended "finishing" schools. But whereas a boy went off to one of the "public" schools run by a private foundation that prepared them for Oxford, Cambridge, or one of the Scottish schools such as the University of Edinburgh, girls stayed at home and trained with private tutors. They learned to play instruments, read music, sew and embroider, and often to read and speak French. They also studied literature and other polite subjects that enabled them to successfully play hostess and educate their children at home. A successful hostess wielded a great deal of influence. The upper class required constant socialization for making proper marriage matches as well as for making business and political alliances. A wide network of friendships gave members of the landed elite social coherence and a set of shared values that parties, balls, and endless rounds of dinner invitations provided. The hostess invited visitors whom she thought would benefit from each other's company, introduced strangers, began intelligent conversations in small groups, and then circulated among the guests, making sure that isolated guests integrated with the others. Add the management of a large household of servants, advising her husband, often on finances and not infrequently on affairs of state, and the role of upper-class women, though constructed largely for patriarchy, required talent, intelligence, and a great deal of work.

Women in the landed class such as our subject's mother, Lady Palmerston, controlled their own money when they married. Their fathers typically gave them funds, which the women, not the husbands, exclusively managed. This certainly freed women from complete dependence on their husbands and added to their private spending. They also on occasion spent this money to help out their husbands' estates if necessary. The typical upper-class woman faithfully attended services of the Church of England, expressed mildly religious sentiments, but did not share the enthusiasm or strict moral code of middle-class evangelicals. Exceptions to this abounded, of course. Devout, indifferent, worldly, flirtatious, or censorious, religious sentiment depended upon the individual. Marital affairs occurred, certainly more among upper-class women than among the lower classes, if only because they had more opportunity. Upper-class women did not commit adultery as the norm, however. A woman maintained her reputation as a strict maxim and avoided, at all costs, embarrassment to her husband for the good of the family and for the future prospects of her children. Upper-class society overlooked and forgave women and men for almost any violation of social ethics but not for the open exhibition of scandalous behavior.

Victorians assumed, as did the eighteenth-century poet George Lyttelton, that women had one noble vocation in life. He asked in a poem, "What is your sex's earliest, latest care, Your heart's supreme ambition?—To be fair." Paradoxically women were expected to set the moral tone for society, particularly, women in the middle class. Women made the home the center of life, the place of peace and repose where the man who worked as a professional or business owner returned after a hard day's work. The woman oversaw the servants, if only a housemaid and a cook, and taught the children to pray, read, and behave. She supervised the rituals of the house and the purchase of food. She entertained at dinner and in the front parlor, the formal part of the middle-class house today called the living room. Men idealized this "angel of the house" and felt the need to provide for and protect women as part of a modern chivalrous code of honor. Women worked in one sphere and men in another. Men often looked to women to set the moral tone. She guarded her own virtue and tried through love and feminine charm to guard the virtue of her husband. Much of the "prudish" tone that later generations assigned to Victorian society flowed from the highly evangelical, religious, and dutiful character of the middle-class woman. An upper-class woman sometimes divorced, but middle-class women divorced with great difficulty. Society utterly rejected a middle-class woman discovered in an affair. Popular literature described such a wife as a "fallen woman," a fate "worse than death."

Women in the lower class shared many of the same responsibilities for running the household as those in the middle class, but they did not hire extra help and accomplished all the work themselves. Unlike women in the middle and landed classes, a woman in the working class often worked for pay to supplement the family budget. Sometimes she worked by spinning thread, tailoring, or taking on piecework, where the owner of a textile business paid her for assembling and sewing garments. Women and children often worked in the textile mills. Women needed this extra money to help the household survive. In addition, they cleaned and cooked and raised the children without servants. Many lower-class women did not marry at all because they had difficulty finding suitable mates that made enough money to raise a family. Many single women became domestic servants and worked as maids, scullery maids, cooks, and wet nurses.

The Arts

Romanticism and Utilitarianism enriched art in the Victorian era and colored the tenor of artistic expression. Romanticism began in the early phases of the Industrial Revolution as a reaction against industrial society. As urban areas grew, factories sprouted across the midlands of England, and more of the population lived in city areas. A reaction set in. This reaction, called the Romantic movement, did not spread much among the working class because they did not have the leisure time to indulge in imagining an escape from their predicament by reading poetry and literature and viewing sculptures and paintings. Poets such as Blake, Wordsworth, Coleridge, Byron, Shelly, and Keats all emphasized romantic images of nature, and pictured the countryside as the repository of repose, beauty, and virtuous living. Imagining the exotic art and nature of the British empire also fed into Romanticism. For the most part the readers of these poets hailed from the growing middle class who dreamed of escaping from the toil of their work and the cramped spaces of the cities.

This romantic tendency to look at the past followed in the footsteps of many enlightenment philosophers who modeled their critique of civic society on an appeal to nature. It also included a fascination with things Greek and Roman, where the artist carefully blended love of beauty and nature with self-control and duty. But Romantic artists found a particular fascination with the Middle Ages. Many painters in this tradition tried to bring back the gothic motifs that gave religious meaning and coherence to life before the modern age.

Romanticism fused with Utilitarianism. John Stuart Mill, the most prominent British philosopher of his age and a founder of Utilitarianism, serves as a good example. Many contemporaries accused him of being a logic-chopping machine, but he in fact argued that the strict ideas of political economy and liberty as laid down by his predecessor, Jeremy Bentham, should include values of the spiritual life and an appreciation for beauty and meaningful relationships. Mill, like Bentham, argued for "the greatest good for the greatest number," which meant in practice that legislation should be determined by the very practical test of whether it benefited, or pleased, the most people. He also argued in his book *On Liberty* for laws that maximized personal choice and individual freedom,

. . . the only purpose for which power can be rightfully exercised over any member of a civilized community, against his will, is to prevent harm to others. His own good, either physical or moral, is not sufficient warrant. He cannot rightfully be compelled to do or forbear because it will be better for him to do so, because it will make him happier, because, in the opinion of others, to do so would be wise, or even right. . . . The only part of the conduct of anyone, for which he is amenable to society, is that which concerns others. In the part which merely concerns himself, his independence is, of right, absolute. Over himself, over his own body and mind, the individual is sovereign.

Though concerned with the rights of the minority in a democratic system, Mill's practical utilitarian thought affected artistic expression. Artists tended to create beautiful works that taught an object lesson and backed up the moral system of the middle class. The painter Augustus Egg for instance painted pictures illustrating the devastation that occurred when a woman betrayed her husband. Novelists illustrated the same blend of romance and utility. Charles Dickens, the premier novelist of the mid-Victorian age, attempted true-to-life portraits of the devastation of industrialism. His novels promoted romantic ideas, and while not necessarily a utilitarianism, argued a reform of manners and behavior that could make a difference in the life of the unfortunate, such as the reform of orphanages and prison systems.

Industrialization, the impulse to reform, and the flowering of Romantic culture in the early and mid-Victorian period go a long way toward explaining Britain's influence on the world. Industrialization gave Britain the economic means of expanding its empire of trade and influence, while its cultural renaissance in the nineteenth century enforced a conviction that the superiority of its civilization conferred on the British a sober responsibility to govern and civilize the less accomplished peoples of the world. Though some Britons questioned the economic utility of the empire, few questioned the moral obligation to maintain and expand the empire for the good of others. Palmerston represented these ideals in his life and policies, and when he entered high office, he made decisions based on these values, which, in turn, affected the shape and contour of the modern world.

2

The People's Aristocrat

Palmerston greatly influenced the nineteenth century but remained in many ways a thoroughly eighteenth-century character. His ancestors served the Tudor royal family in the 1500s and then sided with the parliamentary rebellion in the English Civil War, gaining from Oliver Cromwell grants of land seized from Irish rebels during an uprising. His father, the second Viscount Palmerston, collected rent from his Irish tenants. His father embodied an eighteenth-century aristocrat in every way: he visited his estates in Ireland only once, he loved the city life, and he spent most of his time—when not traveling abroad—in London. He sat in Parliament and counted as his friends the leading cultural lights of the day such as the actor David Garrick, the painter Sir Joshua Reynolds, the historian Edward Gibbon, the famous scientist and president of the Royal Society Sir Joseph Banks, and the great literary lion and author of the first English dictionary, Dr. Samuel Johnson. The elder Palmerston collected art and spent huge sums on paintings and sculpture, traveling to Europe primarily to shop for cultural treasures. His son imbibed the London atmosphere of a world empire of business and a cultural bazaar where great minds met together in coffee shops and debated ideas passionately.

While France boasted a larger population and an elite society that until the French Revolution luxuriated in an aristocratic culture, the British had the largest empire of any nation, a powerful and rapidly expanding commercial class, and a capital city that pulsated with entrepreneurial energy. Alongside the docks on the river Thames rose a forest of masts from sailing vessels that visited every part of the world—the Spanish empire, Africa, India, the Far East, the North American colonies. London had three thousand coffee shops, distinguished less by location and product than by the subject matter under discussion. Writers of poetry, novels, and philosophy met scientists and inventors. Many writers received money from their literary productions. But many of the fields under discussion had not yet developed into professions, and enthusiasts of philosophy, for instance, promoted their ideas as amateurs, without pay. In this world, the coffee shop partially broke down class distinctions (by no means completely) and the aristocrat often listened and debated with the rising merchant class. Though the coffee-shop crowd shut out the truly poor and uneducated, the middle and upper classes mixed with the aristocracy in the coffeehouses just as they mixed with the aristocracy in the single-minded pursuit of money.

Family Life

The young Palmerston grew up between two styles of life: rural and industrial. A coach ride through England at this time revealed an agricultural economy, a terrain of green rolling hills fenced in with raised earth, hedges, or stone. These fields supported a country population that in Palmerston's youth made up the majority of the populace. Fields, usually rented from a large landowner, surrounded a small village or town with the steeple of the church rising over slate or thatched roofs of stone and timber houses. But though traditional Britain differed much from the burgeoning urban centers, change also affected the countryside. Once regulated by seasons, religious holidays, and church bells, this apparently Arcadian scene received a strain from new forces. At one time traditional associations in the countryside flowed in a vertical relationship with the landowner at the top down to the agricultural worker at the bottom. All knew their place and fit into the great Chain of Being where God had placed them. But radical change in the previous hundred years had wrought transformations that fueled the Industrial Revolution and forever changed Palmerston's England and the world. An agricultural and demographic revolution in the eighteenth century preceded and laid the foundation stones for the roaring engine of the Industrial Revolution. These revolutions made their changes quietly and slowly, like a stream carving out the sides of a chalky bank.

After 1660 the agricultural and demographic revolution framed the country life of the Palmerston family. The agricultural revolution began two centuries before his birth at the end of the religious civil wars in Britain and raised production for a number of reasons. Using a legal tool called "enclosure," landlords began to abolish the old open-field system where peasants farmed a strip of land and paid the landlord with a percentage of the crop. Landlords gained the right from Parliament (called a "private act") to enclose their land, which meant that rather than collect rents from a greater number of small farmers, they reallocated the land into larger plots, abolishing or buying out the rights of small farmers and cottagers to common areas like grazing fields and forests. By farming the land themselves or renting the land out to farmers in bigger plots, as well as establishing roads and draining swamps and other improvements, the agricultural production of the land swelled. The small farmers were usually paid for their small plots of land if they had documentation. They could either join the new efficient plots by sub-renting from the lord or, as was the case with most, offer themselves as laborers working for the larger farms where they had once farmed their own land as their ancestors had done for generations. The English countryside, and much of lowland Scotland, Ireland, and Wales gained a neat, romantic, hedged look, with efficient and prosperous farms. Many thousands of people, however, who were no longer tied to the land of their ancestors, moved into the growing, crowded, and smoky cities to obtain jobs as laborers in the new factories. In this way the forces behind the picturesque British countryside fed the wealth of the Industrial Revolution with new workers, increased food, and provided greater income for the landowners.

The rich alternated their life between town and country, and so did the young Palmerston's family. They held most of their land in Ireland. This advantage only dawned slowly on the young Palmerston. Later in life it meant that though inheriting a title of lord he could still sit in the lower house of Parliament. English, Scottish, and Welsh lords took their seats in the upper house as a matter of course. But according to the terms of the 1801 Act of Union that merged the Kingdom of Ireland with the United Kingdom of Britain, the Peers of Ireland elected twenty-eight temporal lords and four spiritual lords to the House of Lords. All the other Irish lords had to seek their seat by election in the lower House of Commons. That meant that though a member of the landed elite, Palmerston could represent a district in the lower house, where the real political power lay. Though most of Palmerston's land lay in Ireland, the main family residence, Broadlands, was located in the county of Hampshire in England, and the London town house sat in Hanover Square.

Palmerston's mother, Lady Palmerston, bore another son besides Henry, named William, born 1788, and also three daughters, Fanny in 1786, Mary in 1789, and Elizabeth in 1790. Mary, however, died while young. Palmerston thus grew up in an active family, and remained close to his brother and surviving sisters for the rest of his life. After she dispatched Henry to Harrow, followed by his brother William, Lady Palmerston attended to her salon and hosted distinguished guests at their London home in Hanover Square and at Broadlands. Palmerston's father, in spite of his aristocratic tastes and habits, did not abound in money because he had great difficulty collecting his rents from Ireland after Irish tenants rose up in rebellion in 1798. This meant that during much of Palmerston's early childhood the family lived on less than the normal aristocratic budget. Sending his son off to school, his father reminded him of the necessity of keeping a reasonable budget, particularly keeping away from excessive drinking and gambling.

School Life

Work filled the void where no husband could be found. One poet, Lord Lyttelton, advised that a woman should "Seek to be good, but aim not to be great" and that her greatest station in life "is retreat" in the home of her husband. Palmerston's sisters, Fanny and Elizabeth, did not attend school. School prepared the boy to play the man's role of ambition and action in the world. Palmerston attended "public school," which means he attended a school sponsored by a private foundation. Schools like Harrow, prepared the sons of the landed elite and the sons of richer businessmen. They studied the Greek and

Roman classics in preparation for taking a leading role in the life of the nation. Palmerston described his studies in a letter to a friend. He read "Caesar, Terence, Ovid, Homer, the Greek Testament, and a collection of Greek epigrams," and after the holidays picked up "Virgil, Horace and some more." He also studied mathematics and excelled with figures, which served him well later in life when he balanced departmental budgets.

At eleven years of age a school friend, Francis Hare, visiting the town of Bologna, Italy, wrote young Palmerston a letter that gives a glimpse into a future classicist and teacher who remained Palmerston's friend until his death in Sicily in 1840.

> I hope, dear Harry, that you continue always well, and that you profit much at school, both in Greek and Latin. I make you this wish, as I think it the very best that a true friend can make, and I think I ought to believe that you place me in this number.
>
> I hope you take no part in those vices which are common to a pubic school, such as I suppose Harrow, as swearing and getting drunk; but I imagine the son of a gentleman so well taught cannot partake in things like these.
>
> Pray give a kiss to each of your two amiable sisters but particularly to Fanny, and tell her to write me a letter whenever you answer mine. I still persist in my opinion of never marrying, and I suppose you think the same, as you must have read, as well as myself, of the many faults and vices of women.
>
> Perhaps I at Bologna may have learnt more Greek than you, and that you at Harrow may know best how to fight with your fist; however, if you challenge me I shall not hesitate to accept, for I remember I am an English boy, and will behave like a brave one. Pray salute for me Willie Ponsonby, whom you and I knew in Italy. Billy desires not to be forgotten by you. I have no more time for writing, so shall only add that I shall wait for your answer with impatience. I protest myself, with all my heart, your most affectionate friend.

Palmerston's answer shows how much he shared his friend's ideals, with a notable exception on the vices of women,

> Dear Hare,—I have just recovered from the measles, which, however, I have had very slightly, and am now very well. I am sincerely obliged to you for your kind wish, and trust that I make as much progress as boys in my situation at school generally do.
>
> . . . I suppose however, that you have made considerable progress in your learning, more than is perhaps in my power. . . I am perfectly of your opinion concerning drinking and swearing, which, though fashionable at present, I think extremely ungentlemanlike; as for getting drunk I can find no pleasure in it. I am glad to see that though educated in Italy you have not forgot old England. Your letter brings to my mind the pleasant time I spent in Italy, and makes me wish to revisit the country I am now reading so much about; and when I am

sucking a sour orange, purchased by perhaps eight biochi, I think with regret upon those which I used to get in such plenty in Italy; and when eating nasty things nicknamed sausages, envy you at Bologna, who perhaps are now feasting off some nice ones.

. . . I cannot agree with you about marriage, though I should be by no means precipitate about my choice. Willy is come to Harrow, and sends his love to you. I send you no news, as I know none. Adieu! Believe me ever your affectionate friend.

Harrow had become fashionable. The aristocratic youth at Harrow lived well and tended to drink heavily and fight. But the university's schools did foster independence and taught boys how to regulate each other's behavior—while boys appealed ultimately to the authorities of the schools, they prided themselves on keeping order among themselves. Life at Harrow painted a miniature portrait of the boys' futures. They read, they debated among themselves, played cricket, drank, hunted rabbits, and sometimes gambled. Stories recounted many years later about Palmerston at Harrow describe him as delicate of health yet plucky with a pleasant personality. He gained a taste for public performance at Harrow, inspired particularly by the headmaster, Joseph Drury. He claimed that the magical speaking of the headmaster so enriched his audience that boys broke the rules of the school merely to be scolded by Drury's superb oratory.

Other influences colored Palmerston's childhood. The French Revolution gave him a graphic impression of "the mob" that he retained the rest of his life and may have dramatically affected his politics. He may also have absorbed some of the views of his father on the subject. In search of art for his collection, Viscount Palmerston took his family to France in 1792. Palmerston's father already had an aversion to the revolution. Earlier in Europe he saw mobs hanging aristocrats in the street and burning down their mansions. He agreed with his friend the great conservative parliamentarian Edmund Burke that the revolution destroyed rather than gave birth to liberty. According to a letter he wrote to his wife, Lady Palmerston, he witnessed an aristocrat pulled from his chateau in Lyons, cut to pieces, roasted, and eaten. These graphic horror stories surely had an effect on the young Palmerston's politics.

The young Palmerston had his own experiences to count on. In the beginning of summer 1792, the French revolutionary forces, led by Danton, took control of Paris and prepared to disarm the Swiss guards that protected the king and queen of France. Soon after the Palmerston family arrived, Louis XVI and Marie Antoinette received them at court. While the meeting went off pleasantly enough, the family could feel the apprehension at court—the revolutionary guards would soon march on the palace and place the king and queen under house arrest. Lady Palmerston, showing more sense than her husband, hurried them away from Versailles and back into Paris to gain travel documents from the revolutionary government. Their suite of carriages managed to cross the border out of France, but not before Palmerston saw for himself the chaotic mobs threatening violence, smoke billowing from burning houses, and bodies hanging from lampposts. Soon after, the revolutionaries imprisoned and then killed Louis XVI, in January 1793, and Marie Antoinette in October 1793.

The great conservative parliamentarian Edmund Burke expressed the horror of the British public at the regicide. In Reflections on the Revolution in France, he wrote that he had never seen a more delightful vision than the queen of France,

> glittering like the morning star, full of life and splendor, and joy. . . . Little did I dream that I should have lived to see disasters fallen upon her in a nation of gallant men, in a nation of men of honor, and of cavaliers. I thought ten thousands swords must have leaped from their scabbards to avenge even a look that threatened her with insult. But the age of chivalry is gone. That of sophisters, economists, and calculators, has succeeded; and the glory of Europe is extinguished for ever.

A new age had indeed arrived and Europeans everywhere felt the change. But the Palmerstons escaped France and traveled to a warmer climate in Italy, where the landed class still found a friendly reception. There Viscount Palmerston continued buying art and attending dinner parties. In Italy young Palmerston began lessons in Italian, a language in which he later gained fluency, and gained in addition a love of the Bologna sausages he had earlier imagined his young friend Hare enjoying. His trip home through northwestern Europe gave him— for one so young—a remarkably broad exposure to European culture and politics. The trip served another purpose as well—it replaced the normal "European tour" when he graduated from Harrow. Normally after school the young men of the landed elite toured the mainland of Europe before training at Oxford or Cambridge. It served as a "finishing school" and gave exposure to other great cities such as Paris, Rome, and Athens, as well as exposure to superb collections of classical art. Europeans, often at war, nonetheless kept a conception of "Christendom" alive, sharing a single Christian faith with similar cultural roots. Therefore, even in war most Europeans maintained a chivalrous respect for travelers so that they traveled in relative safety as they visited their neighbors throughout the continent.

The Ideas of Adam Smith

The war on the continent denied the traditional grand tour to Palmerston. When he finished at Harrow, Napoleon was successfully subduing the great powers of Europe, rendering the grand tour out of the question. So instead of going east to Paris he traveled north to Edinburgh at sixteen years of age to study under the famous Scottish professor Dugald Stewart, a philosopher in the mold of the famous economist Adam Smith. Here he stayed three years, during which, he admitted, "the foundation of whatever useful knowledge and habits of mind I possess" was laid. Palmerston made an impression of being charming, intelligent, industrious, and meek.

Intellectuals considered the universities in Scotland more rigorous than Oxford and Cambridge, and in the eighteenth century Scotland had undergone a renaissance of learning, producing, among their greatest examples, the philosophers Adam Smith and later David Hume. Palmerston's father, in spite of being strapped for cash because of the difficulty collecting Irish rents, and with funds further exhausted from art purchases, nonetheless paid the substantial sum of four hundred pounds a year for the professor's services in the "Northern Athens," as Edinburgh was known in the late eighteenth century. Dugald Stewart hosted other sons of English noblemen in his house, including Henry Petty, soon to become the Marquis of Lansdowne, whose career became inseparable from the history of the Whig party in the mid-Victorian period.

Why would a conservative Tory send his son into the hotbed of Whig thinking that promoted the new free market ideas of the manufacturing class, what they called at the time, "political economy"? For one thing Viscount Palmerston wanted a rigorous education for his son and may have always had in mind for the youth—with his training in Italian and French—a diplomatic career. Second, both his father and his mother had faith in their son holding to Tory principles. Lady Malmesbury, a close friend of the family, had no doubt that the young Palmerston would stick to his principles. "A boy of nineteen may be seduced by a fair face, or led into gaming, or dancing, or racing, but nobody at that age cares about politics that is worth a farthing." While in fact, young Palmerston did care about politics, she predicted rightly that he posed little danger of falling into radical politics.

But if he proved safe from the radical ideas of human liberty promoted by the French Revolution, he did absorb ideas of political economy from Professor Stewart. He scribbled copious notes gleaned from his lessons. And while Stewart avoided political discussion with his students, at the dinner table he discussed freely his ideas about the best possible economic system. Palmerston absorbed these ideas with enthusiasm. For the rest of his life the ideas of Adam Smith taught him by Stewart guided his thinking and affected his public policy.

Adam Smith predicated his work on a set of assumptions about human nature prominent in the eighteenth century. In particular, his views on human nature and the "invisible hand" of the conscience formed Smith's ideas on the working of the market. The idea of the "invisible hand" became a powerful metaphor that guided—and still guides—much public policy. Smith argued in The Theory of Moral Sentiments (1759) that selfishness rules individuals and society—that people act in their own best interests. People desire money for the esteem that money brings—it brings approval from others. The conscience expresses the awareness that people have of the group and the standards of the group. The conscience equates to an "invisible hand" that guides our actions as if a group of people watched all of our thoughts and our behaviors. When Smith wrote his Inquiry into the Nature and Causes of the Wealth of Nations (1776) he used this conception of the invisible hand to explain how the marketplace works. Like the conscience, the market allocates resources in the most efficient way through the collected choices people make. Further, in a free market, people regulate their own behavior through the invisible hand of conscience to keep the system from becoming overly competitive, vicious, and exploitive.

These powerful ideas fit the ambitions of a rising business class and appealed to all levels of society, including many large landowners such as Palmerston. The ideas contained in the book had definite effects on public policy. For example, Smith believed that societies progressed through steps from hunting, pastoral, agricultural, and then to the commercial stage. This commercial stage constituted the highest. Adam Smith's ideas contained radical challenges to traditional societies. The landed elite in Britain, indeed around the world, represented to Smith a legitimate stakeholder in the marketplace. But many of Smith's followers went further and argued that the political leadership of the agricultural age represented an outdated stage of human development. That meant that when a better and new age came into its own, then a new political class would rise to power with it. This new age loomed on the horizon. Palmerston, though a representative of agricultural elite, would nonetheless consciously promote foreign policy that reflected the ideas of Smith and Stewart. Economic policy that resulted in a new class of political leadership—a changing of the guard at the top—constitutes one of Palmerston's enduring influences on global history outside of Britain. He proved far more supportive of the traditional landed elite in his own country however, than he did in other parts of the world.

Palmerston learned much about free trade in Scotland. He made an earnest and attentive student in the city of Edinburgh where Whigs articulated percipient arguments for free trade. While staying with professor Stewart, Palmerston created the impression of a very mild-mannered, civil, and gentle human being. He studied hard, hunted, hiked, socialized with his friends, ate moderately to please his mother and, to please his father, took rhubarb pills every day for his health.

Family crises punctured the calm intellectual atmosphere, however. Near the end of his stay with the professor, his father took ill at an inn outside London. Palmerston rushed south but his carriage arrived too late. While on the road, his father died of cancer of the throat. Arriving at the inn, not knowing the truth, a servant remarked about his father's sudden death. Young Palmerston had not at all expected it. Although he knew his father had health problems, he did not know his father lay close to death.

He reacted strongly to the death of his father. At only seventeen, he took over the management of large estates. The estates ran on a deficit because of the difficulty the family's agents in Ireland had collecting rents from rebellious tenants. In addition, his father had ran up a huge debt to pay for his lavish living expenses and for the fabulous art collection he built with purchases on his expensive overseas travel. Fortunately for the young Palmerston, now Lord Palmerston himself, a group of competent trustees had been assigned to manage the family's financial affairs until he had "come of age" at twenty-one years old. This proved convenient. Palmerston suffered from depression at his father's death for what his friends and family considered an alarming period of time, and had little energy for managing money.

His father chose trustees with a diplomatic turn. Biographers think that Palmerston's father hoped that his son would choose a diplomatic career, so he appointed James Harris, the Earl of Malmesbury, as trustee and as guardian. Malmesbury had a reputation as a diplomat, serving as England's ambassador to Frederick the Great of Germany and Catherine the Great of Russia. The Viscount Palmerston probably picked Malmesbury with his son's potential career in mind, hoping that such guardians might whet his son's appetite for foreign affairs, and hoping too that they might give his son the contacts and help he needed to pursue a career as a diplomat.

Now that he had finished his term at Professor Stewart's house, Palmerston had to choose a university. Malmesbury favored Cambridge. So did young Lord Palmerston, particularly the college of St. John's, one of a number of colleges that made up the University of Cambridge. Malmesbury liked St. John's because other aristocratic youths from Harrow attended there, and Palmerston because St. John's boasted a liberal policy that allowed undergraduates to keep horses, a forbidden practice in much of the rest of the university. The university did not require aristocrats to study, for the elite attended Cambridge or Oxford as a finishing school rather than as training for serious scholarship or a particular profession. In fact, the university did not require aristocratic students to take exams at all. But Palmerston, once at Cambridge, perhaps inspired by the very serious academic environment of Edinburgh in Dr. Stewart's household, insisted on attending lectures, studying hard, and sitting for the exams. He threw himself into a debating club created by a few friends, "the Speculative" and took all aspects of life at university seriously. He even served in a local militia that formed on the expectation of an invasion by Napoleon—an invasion that never happened. Unlike many aristocratic undergraduates, Palmerston was not idle.

Oxford and Cambridge at this time harbored some of the most prolific minds of the world, and aristocratic families sent their sons to these hoary seats of learning to intermingle with their own class and with scholars of international repute. Yet the famous historian Gibbon earlier described these two schools as "pleasant . . . unprofitable pools of slumber." In Parliament Palmerston joked years later—with some exaggeration—that his primary pastime at Cambridge besides boating was forgetting all he learned at Edinburgh. But while the universities lacked rigor, and required no exams for aristocratic students, these ancient citadels of learning still produced finely trained minds, particularly in the classics of literature and theology. Professors stressed the cardinal importance of grueling fields such as history, Greek, Latin, philosophy, logic, and rhetoric, which developed superb skills in writing, thinking, and speaking, all of which prepared graduates for the professional life of the clergy, law, and the Parliament. The busy social life included a meeting of the minds in each college where professors and students sat for common meals. The conversations over the meals—conversations that highly prized wit and learning—prepared

Palmerston more than the lectures and tutors. He spent his time well: going to bed at one in the morning and rousing himself at seven.

While he seemed to enjoy the intellectual work at the university and drinking with friends (moderately, for he abhorred drunkenness), the boating, hunting, horse riding, and dinners in the commons and the rooms of his colleagues, tragedy and sorrow punctuated his time at the university. His mother died of cancer, only three years after the death of his father, just before he sat for his exams. This happened in 1805, and now the young Palmerston had on his shoulders the care of his family as well as the management of the estates. These events made him more serious about getting on with his life ambitions.

Parliament

He discerned that Parliament lay in his future, but suffered misgivings about such an early run. Events hastened the circumstances that made it possible to enter Parliament. In 1803, England, after a brief period of peace, plunged back into war with France. The British turned naturally to the prime minister William Pitt to lead them. But in January1806, Pitt died. Pitt had represented Cambridge, and parliamentary procedure required a by-election to fill his place. Palmerston had obviously impressed the dons at St. John's College with his ability and temperament, and they must have sensed that this well-connected young man would someday cut a figure in the politics of the nation. So they invited him to run for the seat in Parliament with their full support. This flattered Palmerston greatly, and he gladly accepted the offer.

He campaigned as a Conservative, (the term "Tory" was then slowly coming into use to describe a conservative member of Parliament) the party of his father and, for the most part, of his class, the large landowners. Conservatives tended to support rural values and institutions, including the privileged role of the Church of England in society. Palmerston campaigned hard for the seat, but the political tide ran against the Tories and toward the Whigs. Agitation against slavery had made slavery an important issue with growing numbers of business- and evangelical-minded Whigs, who often supported the manufacturing interests against the landowners, and tended to support "dissenters" who held church membership outside the Church of England. Many Tories as well thought that Parliament needed to halt the much publicized brutalities of the slave trade. Palmerston lost to the Whig candidate, Lord Henry Petty, later Lord Lansdowne, a fellow student at Professor Stewart's house, senior by a few years to Palmerston. Though he lost the battle, the campaign gave him a taste of politics.

He ran again in the general election of 1807 for the same Cambridge seat and gained the official backing of the Tory party, not merely his teachers at St. John's College. But again he lost, this time by only three votes. This close loss occurred because of the voting format: each voter cast two votes for this seat. The Cambridge seat returned not one but two candidates, and voters had two votes to cast. He could vote "straight," which is to say, he could vote for the two party members put forward by his party, or the voter could split his votes and vote for a member of his own party and then a member of another party. Or lastly, the voter could "plump" his vote, that is, vote for the one candidate the voter liked but hold back his other vote because—as sometimes happened—he did not like the other candidate. It took, therefore, some planning and negotiating with other candidates to get them to give their "plumpers," that is, their second vote. Since Palmerston had promised his plumpers to Vicary Gibbs, another candidate, the voters who lined up behind Gibbs pledged to return the favor. Many, however, did not.

One reason for this may have been Palmerston's principled stand on toleration of religious dissent. He rather courageously supported removing disabilities against Catholics; that is, allowing them to hold office as members of Parliament and to attain high rank in the military based on merit, a position that the Tory party on the whole—and King George III—opposed. Palmerston controverted his party on the issue, but the party agreed not to press Palmerston. Even while this gained him some credibility with the Whigs, he still lost again.

His determination impressed his former guardian, Lord Malmesbury. Deciding to intervene in the career of his former ward and also for his own son, Malmesbury contacted the Irwin family that controlled a pocket borough in Horsham Sussex. A "pocket borough" was a small voting district effectively in the control of a single landowner. The viscountess of the borough at one time held sway over the seventy-three electors, and in past elections these electors had voted as the Irwin family wished. She sold her support to Edward Fitzharris, Malmesbury's son, and to Palmerston for fifteen hundred pounds, with another two thousand pounds due if they won and if Parliament declared the election valid after a challenge. A contender for influence, the Duke of Norwalk, wrested the election from the Irwin family after buying property in the area. While Palmerston was elected for Horsham in 1806, he was deprived of his seat on petition to Parliament in 1807. Thus Palmerston lost his fifteen hundred pounds and the election.

He ran again to represent Cambridge, and lost again. But a seat once held by his father salvaged his ambitions for office. Newport, a borough in the Isle of Wight, under the patronage of a Sir Leonard Holmes, offered the seat to Palmerston, as he had to Palmerston's father years earlier. There was only one requirement: Palmerston must never visit the district. Holmes wanted no competition for influence. So at last Palmerston entered office—not in a successful appeal to the people in a contested election but by patronage, in a voting district controlled by a local landlord, called a "rotten borough."

His high position in society helped him gain his first important office. Just before his election to Parliament, Lord Malmesbury used his influence to have Palmerston selected as a Lord of the Admiralty, a position that was considered a good start for young men beginning their political career. In reality, Palmerston had little to do other than sign his name on official documents. As a "Junior Lord," Palmerston listened more than he spoke at the early meetings for this office. The position, though, gave him a little more influence in Parliament, which he used eventually to good advantage. Parliamentarians and party leaders watched closely the first speech, always a momentous occasion, called the "maiden speech," to judge the potential of the new member. Wisely, Palmerston chose to speak on a topic that had a connection to his position on the admiralty board. In 1807, George Canning filled the office of foreign secretary and authorized a swift military intervention into Copenhagen to capture the Danish fleet and keep it from falling into the hands of Napoleon. The Whigs fulminated at this intervention into a neutral country. Canning also refused to disclose the information he had obtained that justified the intervention, claiming he would jeopardize the safety of his sources. After one member made a withering attack on Canning, Palmerston rose to make his maiden speech.

Palmerston began by stating that it would have been gross impropriety of ministers like Canning to reveal their sources of information, particularly when the strictest promise of secrecy pried the intelligence from vulnerable sources. The honor of England hung in balance. To disclose the source of information would also destroy any future success in gaining information. Perhaps, he reasoned, if the gentleman MP's on the other side of the house possessed no information for the necessity of the attack, then the government would produce the desired evidence. But the situation in Europe made the justification clear: Europe stood in great danger of being reduced to a system of vassals, the sovereigns of the states mere puppets of Napoleon. The law of nations—the legal precedents that European legal philosophers generally agree upon—made attacks on neutral countries illegal. But in this case, self-preservation dictated the necessity of naval action. Neutral Denmark lay weak at the feet of France, ready for Napoleon to strike and merely appropriate the Danish fleet. Did the law of nations apply to Napoleon, an aggressor seeking to dominate all of Europe? The crown prince of Denmark had the chance to side with Britain, and "yet he would not listen to any overture from this country for his security and protection." Therefore, he left himself open to domination from France and would have become an instrument against Great Britain. The foreign secretary, he argued, struck a justified and necessary blow against the dictator of Europe and for the preservation of England and of liberty by sinking the Danish fleet.

The speech laid down a precedent for how Palmerston would handle crises in the future. First, laws should govern the conduct of nations and their leaders. Second, in case of war or extraordinary hardship, the law of survival should overrule the laws that govern the normal conduct of nations. If the basic interests of Britain conflicted with the first principle, then national interest must come first.

In a letter to his sister Elizabeth he ruminated on the aftermath of his speech,

> My dear Elizabeth,—You will see by this day's paper that I was tempted by some evil spirit to make a fool of myself for the entertainment of the House last night; however I thought it was a good opportunity of breaking the ice, although one should flounder a little in doing so, as it was impossible to talk any very egregious nonsense upon so good a cause. . . .

He offered one complaint: "The papers have not been very liberal in their allowance of report to me."

As his first speech showed, he strained honestly to apply a fair, nonpartisan rule of law, but then he suspended such considerations when and if he considered the interests of Britain at stake. This formula made his policies pragmatic: they appealed to higher ideals and yet almost always had a practical payoff for British power and trade. This Janus-faced policy—one face looking toward fair play and openness, the other toward self-interest and power—set a new standard for leadership in modern democracies in the future. The Palmerstonian method is still the preferred approach in most democracies today. It was not that leaders never before dressed up self-interest in altruism or a higher cause. Rather, Palmerston's example led to a formula of conduct: officials and politicians first appeal to a higher cause overridden only when self-interest dictates.

To the modern mind this seems unprincipled, but at this time only Great Britain and the United States had an "opposition" party that appealed to higher principles of conscience and subsequently made demands upon the government to act against the best interest of the country and in the interest of a higher morality. While contemporary politicians often express altruistic sentiments today, often with dubious sincerity, the evangelical temper of British and American society introduced reform-minded issues of conscience into the public theater of discussion—a conscience informed by the evangelical need to hold others to a higher law based principally on the egalitarian ideas found in the New Testament and secularized into rational systems of thought in the Enlightenment. Palmerston resisted, or at least tempered this evangelical impulse in politics.

Part of the secret of his political success lay in his remarkable ability to mollify the evangelical element of public opinion without alienating the rest of society. He accomplished this feat by creating a rhetorical approach to foreign policy that explicated the grab for British power, wealth, and prestige in terms of altruism. The military only aggressively tackled an opposing force for a higher moral purpose, whether for responsible government or for the moral uplift of free trade. He explained to his attentive parliamentarians that self-interest only bestowed urgency to actions motivated by virtue. Palmerston formulated this modified evangelicalism for the British public and thus made an almost impossibly difficult evangelical code of conduct palatable to evangelical critics and to the operation of efficient government.

In his own life, he certainly overrode evangelical principles. Palmerston was a Christian gentleman, not an evangelical. That meant that socializing with members of his own class—what we would now call "networking"—filled a large part of his life. He became known more for the quality and variety of his wines than for his ambition. He soon developed the reputation of "Lord Cupid" in his private life because of his epicurean taste and affairs with women. To be single in the Regency period, and a member of the ruling class, meant socializing on a large scale; Palmerston did not fail in this respect.

The classical education that Palmerston received found an outlet in conversation as well as in Parliament. The upper class socialized for cohesion, exchange of information, alliances, marriages, and uniformity of ethics. In practice this involved much conversation at parties, dinners, dances, clubs, coffeehouses, hunting parties, and while traveling. A Christian gentleman had to prove himself intelligent, witty, conversant in classical literature, and, if possible, humorous. He needed to converse easily in music, the arts, and literature and to ride a horse comfortably and gracefully, handling deftly the "ribbons" (reins) of a carriage and shooting guns accurately. The British landed elite merged the ideal of a well-rounded Renaissance man with the Roman emphasis on manly virtue.

In reality, few lived up to all of these attainments—many preferred hunting to discussing poetry. Some, such as the politician Peel, a gifted orator, never felt comfortable riding a horse: in fact Peel died riding in St. James Park when his horse fell and crushed him underneath. But for the most part, the landed elite were not professionals who made their living by specialized labor but generalists who lived off rent payments by tenants and income from investments. Many did practice medicine, serve as priests, and teach at Oxford and Cambridge, but younger sons tended to fill this role, while the first sons managed their estates and their financial investments, socializing furiously. Marriage and relationships with peers yielded higher returns than working professions when inherited wealth cascaded from generation to generation.

Though Palmerston was a social success—if not a celebrity of society—many also thought him dull. His peers regarded him as a hardworking bureaucrat and a low-ranking politician with an active but uninspiring social life. In other words, Palmerston's contemporaries viewed him as a charming lightweight who, due to his aristocratic rank and fortune, made good husband material but otherwise ought not be taken too seriously.

He spent much of his time at Almack's, considered the most exclusive club in the country. Only club members of the opposite sex proposed candidates for membership—which gives some idea of the social purposes of the club. At the time Palmerston entered it seven lady patronesses ruled it as a private kingdom—denying some very highly placed aristocrats like the Duchess of Bedford and accepting others—all on the basis of personal likes and dislikes. He befriended three of the seven patronesses: Lady Cowper, who later became his wife; Madame de Lieven, a Russian countess married to the Russian ambassador; and Lady Jersey. Palmerston may have had affairs with any or all of these three ladies, but there is no conclusive evidence of this—though he had close friendships with all of them, and he certainly loved Lady Cowper enough to marry her after Lord Cowper died.

But in between attending the theater, entertaining in his home, hunting at Broadlands, and socializing, he also found time to reform his estates in Ireland. When he first toured his Irish estates, something his father rarely did, the ragged peasant farmers and degraded condition of the land appalled him. Roads were abysmal, schools were few and underfunded, and the small farmers met him on the roadside to beg him to allow them to pay their rents directly to him and to eliminate the middleman farmers who abused them. Palmerston responded by reforming the estates, getting rid of the midsized farmers, setting up schools with Catholic teachers—a generous concession to the religion of his tenants—draining fens, improving roads, and building a port to more easily export the goods of his tenants. Given the age, this placed Palmerston in the category of the more progressive and humane landlords.

Secretary at War

Tumultuous politics reflected the uncertainties of society. These events gave rise to another chance for Palmerston to rise in his political career. In 1809 the administration of Lord Portland fell due to a quarrel between George Canning, the foreign secretary, and Lord Castlereagh, the Secretary of State for War. In their anger, they fought a duel. Fortunately for each of them, they both missed. With the fall of the Portland administration, the new administration of Spencer Perceval, a Tory, came into office. Perceval tried to patch together a new administration with new faces. But the leading lights of Canning and Castlereagh each represented a significant faction in the Parliament and neither would serve with the other or support the administration that contained the other. Perceval had no choice but to seek new faces and new blood. This meant turning to talented young men.

In Palmerston's own words,

> It was at that time (the breaking-up of the Portland Ministry) at Broadlands (October, 1809). . . . [I] received a letter from Perceval, desiring me to come to town immediately, as he had a proposal to make to me which he thought would be agreeable: I went up to town, and he offered me the Chancellorship of the Exchequer. I was a good deal surprised at so unexpected an offer, and begged a little time to think of it, and to consult my friends.

Known later for his bold and even reckless foreign policy, Palmerston at this time of his life tiptoed cautiously. When Perceval offered him the position of the Chancellorship of the Exchequer, which would give him administrative control over the treasury—a role that would assist the prime minister with the proposal and defense of the government's budget; a position thus second only in importance to the office of the prime minister—he nonetheless turned it down. Perceval paid the young parliamentarian an immense compliment with the offer. Few hold office of such high magnitude while so young. True, he had made a good impression in Parliament with his maiden speech. He seemed competent and capable. But he did not amaze. No one considered him a prodigy. Perceval, struggling to piece together the members of an administration, turned to Palmerston in desperation. At this point Palmerston could have jumped at the opportunity and made a name for himself early. It would have changed his career by putting him into power and possibly into even higher office much sooner. But he said no. Though "much may be gained, very much also is to be lost" if the job did not go well. As an unpolished speaker Palmerston faced rhetorical lions in the lower house who tore unprepared cabinet ministers apart with ease. If he did not live up to expectations, he would kill his career before it began.

Why did Palmerston fear public speaking and debating? He explained his reticence in a letter to his mentor Lord Malmesbury, "I have always thought it unfortunate for any one, and particularly a young man, to be put above his proper level, as he only rises to fall the lower." He goes on to explain that the upcoming Parliament would be one of "infinite difficulty." England was battling France on land and sea. Napoleon was chasing his enemies around much of Europe. Britain had to bear the financial burden of leading the war effort among shaky and treacherous continental allies and the budget of the country balanced precariously on the edge of bankruptcy. Plus the new Portland ministry, without its veteran debaters and leading men, particularly Canning and Castlereagh, stood on wobbly legs and would be defending itself against an onslaught of seasoned gladiators. The office of Chancellorship of the Exchequer would demand in these trying times, Palmerston wrote, "the talents of Pitt or Fox," who had made their political reputations with forceful eloquence. Although bad speeches were tolerated from members who held little responsibility, bad speeches "would make a Chancellor of the Exchequer exceedingly ridiculous."

Historians debate his caution. Some argue that he missed his chance to play a larger role in society and misspent the next twenty years in the political wilderness. Others, and certainly his mentor Lord Malmesbury, thought the decision showed a rare prescience in a young man. Most would have eagerly jumped at the position, as it offered prestige and power. But recognizing the possible pitfalls of the office took wisdom, and Palmerston may very well have been correct in assessing his chances of failing in the office by taking the public limelight too soon. Palmerston also foresaw the Perceval government would not last long and commented to Malmesbury that "if Perceval cannot find another as good as me for the Exchequer, it's clear, I think, that we [the Tory party] are too weak to stand." Palmerston did not want to risk appearing as a fool in public debate for a government that would not at any rate last very long.

So he accepted another office instead. He took the office of Secretary at War, usually a cabinet post, and at his special request the prime minister downgraded the post to a non-cabinet position. The timidity of taking a lesser office and then requesting that Perceval place him outside the cabinet shocked even his old mentor Malmesbury, who agreed that the first offer might have been too much for a young, inexperienced man but thought that the second office should have been accepted at cabinet level. This reputation for timidity would haunt Palmerston for the next twenty years, until, well into middle age, he burst into the light of British politics and outshone his rivals.

His new position had complicated duties that overlapped with those of the commander in chief. The monarch appointed this latter office that oversaw strategy and promotion of officers. But Palmerston had nothing to do with strategy or the structure of command. There existed a Secretary for War, which oversaw general strategy of the war and the large-scale picture of the military operations. This latter position also had responsibilities as Minister of the Colonies. Yet Palmerston's position of Secretary at War differed vastly in the reach of authority and oversight.

The office workers at the War Office did not find Palmerston as charming as others found him in fashionable society. His subordinates dubbed him "Lord Pumicestone." They considered him finicky and demanding, roughly enforcing rules and routine. Running the Secretary at War office gave him unpleasant administrative responsibilities and, unlike in his previous position as a Jr. Lord of the Admiralty, he actually managed accounts, supervised a staff of bureaucrats, decided delicate issues such as who could get a pension, removed personnel from the payroll, and gave written reports to the prime minister and speeches in Parliament when relevant issues about his department arose. Much of his duties were the work of an accountant. The army had six hundred thousand men in arms; the navy had two hundred thousand sailors and marines, and he ran the organization that oversaw finances for the volunteer militia, the army, and the navy.

He loved his job, not least because he exulted in "the masculine energies of the nation" that made Britain "proud and glorious." He marveled that after fighting Napoleon for fifteen years "we are still able to maintain the war with augmenting force," not to mention a population that kept increasing. But while the larger picture of Britain's strength looked well, the War Office seemed a mess badly in need of a cleaning. An attitude of reform no doubt lay behind much of the animosity that the staff at the War Office felt for Palmerston—it certainly could not have made their job any easier when he moved in. "There is a good deal to be done," he told Malmesbury, and he intended to get working on "interior details" of the War Office to place it on a solid footing. The office operated far behind schedule in arrears of its Regimental Accounts. Worse, he found the finances of the office riddled with corruption at the highest places. Reform meant battling years of inherited habits and inefficient crustations that impeded the administrative gears.

So Palmerston began to clean up the mess. He started with the need to make appointments of qualified, moral individuals who would not take bribes. The opportunity to do so presented itself early. The War Office supervised a number of miscellaneous institutions, one being oversight of various hospitals that housed veterans. The king appointed a new commissioner to manage Chelsea Hospital. Palmerston would then issue the proper warrant as expected. But Palmerston objected. The appointee, a General Delancey, had only a few years earlier been involved in a scandal for skimming public funds as Barrack-Master-General. Appointing him now as commissioner of Chelsea Hospital seemed to reward him for his corrupt activities.

But the king had suggested the appointment, and George III was used to getting his way in matters of patronage. Palmerston appealed to the prime minister, Perceval. The prime minister backed him up against the king. The new Secretary at War won his first fight. His next would prove more difficult. He took on bigger battles, and most of these were with the commander in chief and the Horse Guards. The commander in chief was usually a duke, in this case the Duke of York, brother of King George III. The Horse Guards, the Whitehall headquarters of the British army, was the name of the office that the commander in chief ran, much as the White House, in Washington, D.C., is the official residence and primary workplace for the American president and commander in chief. The commander in chief ran the military, made appointments, and acted as the chief general in charge of the army. When Palmerston decided to reform the War Office, he inevitably collided with the Horse Guards.

One of the changes Palmerston initiated involved the way that the army conducted business. Generals hired aides-de-camps who acted as administrators and secretaries. These aides-de-camps of course needed salaries. A general could have a number of aides, and he could also have a few "ghost positions" where the general received money from the War Office to pay an aide but in fact pocketed the money, substantially augmenting his salary. In addition, the War Office gave colonels money to buy uniforms for their men. Often in fact the colonels purchased the uniforms at a considerable discount from what they claimed they paid and took the money that remained. Palmerston wanted to change this. He insisted that generals should only get money for aides who actually worked for them, and colonels should not get any money at all—the War Office should pay the money directly to the business providing the clothes.

This sounds reasonable today, but for a military establishment still operating on eighteenth-century lines, where corruption was not only extensive but acceptable, Palmerston's actions to reform the War Office raised rabid opposition. Sir David Dundas saw these actions as a gauntlet thrown down at his feet. The Duke of York, the king's brother, had been commander in chief but had taken a leave of office for a short time. Dundas, a Scot serving as interim commander in chief, who fought his way up the ranks by talent and hard work, took offense at Palmerston's reforms, and thought that they materially reduced the authority of the Horse Guards. This, he fumed, would reflect poorly on himself when he returned the trust of office back to the king's brother. So Dundas argued that Palmerston had crossed the lines of authority. In fact, Dundas argued, Palmerston as Secretary at War worked for him, Dundas, the commander in chief. The War Office, he concluded, had become too overbearing and, under Palmerston, overreached.

Even Dundas felt obliged to admit, however, that if a general received money for an aide-de-camp, then that general ought to spend the money on the aide-de-camp and not siphon the money off for himself. Therefore, by way of compromise, the commander in chief would be happy, Dundas informed Palmerston, to inform the War Department if no hire had actually taken place. But as to the issue of the uniforms, he could not compromise at all. To require colonels to give an exact accounting for clothing money was "novel," "extraordinary," and would lead to unforeseen evil consequences. The money should be considered a private transaction between the government and the colonels because the colonels paid for the clothes as if they were for their own wardrobe. The government had as much business asking colonels if they had properly paid the bills for the uniforms as they had asking if they had paid for their hunting boots. With this argument in hand, Dundas appealed to the prime minister for redress, going over Palmerston's head.

Palmerston countered these arguments with his own. Parliament had given authority to the War Office to oversee the expenditures of the military. Dundas made the mistake of thinking that the Secretary at War fit into a hierarchical structure with the commander of chief at the top. Rather, Palmerston's office represented a different hierarchy altogether, one answerable to the representatives of the people, while Dundas answered to the crown. These two powers, and thus these two subordinate positions, created the balance and tension that made up the English constitution. One deals with discipline, the other with finances. If the authority of the two officers overlapped, then they should decide the issue together. Such was not the case here because the issue of the uniforms clearly involved responsibility for military disbursements.

Prime Minister Perceval hesitated to make a decision on the issue and appealed to the prince regent, son of the king. The prince gave a very careful answer, not wishing to upset the delicate relationship between the power of the crown—in this case the commander in chief —and the Parliament—in this case Palmerston. He stated that in the future when the two could not agree they should appeal to the prime minister, who would then discuss the matter with the king. And so the issue rested, a small but remarkable instance of the delicate balance in the gears of the constitutional machinery. This case illustrates how courtesy, custom, and a careful regard for the spirit of balance between the monarchy and the Parliament allowed the constitution of Britain to work. Unlike the written constitution in the United States and in other democratic countries, the "constitution" in Britain, while still a legal force, rests upon mutual understanding and cooperation.

A government that operated with balance and compromise did not mean, however, that cabinet ministries lasted very long. While the British government seemed the most stable in Europe, unexpected events could quickly change the course of politics. On May 11, 1812, an assassin murdered Perceval in the lobby of Parliament before the horrified eyes of lawmakers. After a period of close observation in confinement physicians declared the assassin insane, with no identifiable political agenda. After the death of Perceval, a new prime minister in office, Lord Liverpool (Robert Jenkinson) came to power. Lord Liverpool had been Secretary of State for War and the Colonies. When he formed the next Tory government he offered Palmerston the Secretaryship for Ireland.

This position involved running the day-to-day affairs of the Irish government and stood next in authority to the position of Lord Lieutenant of Ireland, who ruled as viceroy for the king's government. But Palmerston turned the offer down. Next, Liverpool offered it to Robert Peel. Peel had already as a young MP made a positive impact on the Parliament through his exceptional oratory. Ambitious and talented, he seized the opportunity to govern Ireland and proceeded to govern so impartially and with such competence that the public came to expect from Peel a great role in politics. But few thought that of Palmerston. Turning down the Secretaryship for Ireland, Palmerston remained in his position as Secretary at War for another fifteen years. While Peel began his meteoric ascent to power, the informed public thought of Palmerston as a minor official, not without talent, a careful administrator, with growing skills and confidence in public speaking, but with precious little ambition.

Catholic Emancipation

During this long sojourn at the War Office, however, Palmerston undertook some very serious work. He boldly advocated issues that soon made it clear to him that his future lay on the other side of the aisle, and not with the Tories. In 1813 an MP, Mr. Grattan, introduced a measure for Catholic Emancipation. The Glorious Revolution of 1688 guaranteed a protestant monarchy with an established protestant church. The Act of Uniformity (1662) required the use of the Book of Common Prayer for all church services. The Test Acts required that only members of the Church of England could hold a government position. After Charles II, any person holding a public office received communion in the Church of England and took the Oath of Supremacy, which recognized the monarch as the head of the church. The Test Act of 1673 stated, "I [name] do declare that I do believe that there is not any transubstantiation in the sacrament of the Lord's Supper, or in the elements of the bread and wine, at or after the consecration thereof by any person whatsoever." Parliament extended the Act in 1678 and further required the oath taker to abjure the invocation or adoration of the "Virgin Mary, or any other Saint." This meant that sincere Catholics could not take any public office, hold a military position, or sit in Parliament.

Palmerston had little admiration for the Catholic church. His attitudes were a holdover from the eighteenth century, when Rome and Catholic Spain and France had so often been the bitter enemy of England and of constitutional liberty. Yet he spoke strongly in the House of Commons for lifting disabilities against Catholics:

> Is it wise to say to men of rank and property, who, from old lineage or present possessions, have a deep interest in the common weal, that they live in a country where, by the blessings of a free constitution, it is possible for any man, themselves only excepted, by the honest exertion of talents and industry in the avocations of political life, to make himself honoured and respected by his countrymen, and to render good service to the state;—that [Catholics] alone can never be permitted to enter this career; that they may, indeed, usefully employ themselves in the humbler avocations of private life, but that public service they never can perform, public honour they never shall attain? What we have lost by the continuance of this system it is not for man to know; what we might have lost can be more easily imagined. If it had unfortunately happened that, by the circumstances of birth and education, a Nelson, a Wellington, a Burke, a Fox, or a Pitt, had belonged to this class of the community, of what

honours and what glory might not the page of British history have been deprived? To what perils and calamities might not this country have been exposed?

The question is not whether we would have so large a part of the population Catholic or not. There they are, and we must deal with them as we can. It is in vain to think that by any human pressure we can stop the spring which gushes from the earth. But it is for us to consider whether we will force it to spend its strength in secret and hidden courses, undermining our fences and corrupting our soil, or whether we shall at once turn the current into the open and spacious channel of honourable and constitutional ambition, converting it into the means of national prosperity and public wealth.

Parliament dallied long before striking these disabilities. Pitt the Younger tried as prime minister to solve the agitation in Ireland and to bring peace between Britain and Ireland. He proposed to do so by creating the 1800 Act of Union, which created one country out of Ireland and Britain as it had for England and Scotland. He discussed the possibility of including language in the bill that lifted some of the discriminations against Catholics, and wanted to see a separate Catholic relief act accompany this bill. But opposition by Protestants in Ireland, King George III, and very vocal anti-papal segments of the public led to a bill passing Parliament without any emancipation. In this context, Palmerston responded to the call of Mr. Grattan for support. As a Tory, the leading lights of his party expected him to oppose the bill, so he took some real risk in supporting it.

The Tory Lord Liverpool approached Catholic emancipation as an open question, and it was not unheard of for a Tory to back greater freedom for Catholics. But the position taken by Palmerston undercut his support among many Tories who did not wish to see the authority of the Church of England compromised, and who linked the liberties of political freedom with Protestant government. Conservatives worried that Catholic loyalties meant loyalties to Rome and thus to an outside power that would undercut patriotism and trust in the motives of public officials. The opposition of the Tories meant that Grattan's bill did not pass, and it almost knocked Palmerston out of politics altogether. In the next election Palmerston ran for a seat in Cambridge, and only with the support of the Whigs, his political opponents, did he manage to scrape by and hold his seat in Parliament. The experience made him think seriously about his association with the Tories, and he began to feel like an outsider in his own party.

The Napoleonic Wars

The war with France from 1793 to 1815 formed the dramatic backdrop to the early life and career of Palmerston. While Britain battled with France and other powers such as Spain for much of the eighteenth century, this war differed. In many ways it was a conflict between two visions of society, modern and traditional. The new society that arose in France threatened the landed oligarchies of Britain and most of Europe. While the British saw the first developments in the French Revolution as analogous to the Glorious Revolution of 1688, and many welcomed the new constitutional society in France, the French Revolution soon came to divide opinion sharply as the revolution hastened to violent stages that included the mass murders of aristocrats, the establishment of a police state, a new state religion of atheism, and the destruction of beloved cultural loyalties such as Catholicism. The French Revolution thus went far beyond the Glorious Revolution of 1688, and while it inspired many reformers in Britain who wanted the vote given to all males regardless of economic position, it horrified others.

The war with Napoleon had distinct stages. From 1798 to 1802 Britain led a coalition of European powers that Napoleon dismembered blow by blow by winning on the field of battle. In 1802–1803 the Peace of Amiens let France and Britain enjoy a rest from the contest, but from 1803 to 1812 Napoleon towered over Europe as conqueror, losing only the Battle of Trafalgar in 1805 to the British Navy, and then finally in 1812 invading Russia and reeling backward in defeat with only thirty thousand men left, defeated by a coalition of the Great Powers of Europe. He abdicated as emperor, and the allies sent him to exile in Elba, an island in the Mediterranean. He then escaped, launching his "hundred days" recovery of power, in which he marched into Paris, rallying the veterans of his old army, and again took on Europe. This time a coalition of all the major powers together—Britain, Prussia, Austria, and Russia—put his career to an end. The Duke of Wellington defeated Napoleon in the Battle of Waterloo in Belgium, June 18, 1815. Napoleon again resigned from power, and the allies kept him imprisoned until his death in 1821.

Palmerston responded to the terrors of the French Revolution by supporting the Combination Acts and by voting in favor of the Corn Laws in support of the landowning class. But he also agreed with some of the ideas of the French Revolution and preferred—strongly—a free market economy and a society governed constitutionally by a mix of all classes—landowners, the business-minded middle classes, and workers. Biographers have disagreed about where to place Palmerston. Did his peers pigeonhole him as a conservative Tory? A moderate that fit between the Tories and the Whigs? Certainly on his own estates in Ireland he showed himself concerned for the welfare of his tenants, and he took political risks by standing against his own party for Catholic Emancipation. But on other issues, he seemed to share the same fear of unruly mobs demanding democracy as other conservative Tories.

His work at the War Office brought him to the forefront of an issue that helped define him as a conservative. After the end of the war with Napoleon, many expected a respite from heavy taxes, a peace dividend that would cut taxes, downsize the "standing army" of professional soldiers and thus give citizens the leisure to concentrate on the arts of culture and the business of making money rather than war. Peacetime Britain, many proclaimed, needed only a small volunteer militia with a modest standing army.

Henry Broughman, a radical Member of Parliament with great influence, advocated this view and claimed that the Treasury Department should spend less on the army in peacetime than during war. He also complained that the Secretary at War seldom bothered to explain the expenditures of the army to the House of Commons. When Palmerston rose from the bench to answer the accusation we see the early signs of a new Palmerston, confident and awake to his power of persuasion. Addressing the House, he remarked, "I certainly cannot retort upon that honorable gentleman himself [Broughman], namely, that 'he very seldom troubles the House with his observations.'" This remark rather smartly returned the slap to Broughman, by insinuating that if Palmerston spoke too little, Broughman spoke far too much. Palmerston then insisted that he would not, like Broughman, offer a "dissertation on the Constitution" but confine himself to the business at hand—the budget of the army.

He then forcefully argued for the need of a more substantial standing army. For the colonies held before the war Britain required only a small increase in the size of the army—an increase of seven thousand. This was reasonable because during the course of the war the population in most of the empire—Canada for instance—had increased. If an emergency arose in Canada it would take weeks to move additional troops across the Atlantic. But in addition to the greater population in the old colonies, new lands had been added—Ceylon, the Cape, Mauritius, islands in the Caribbean, Malta, and the Ionian archipelago. When the French held these territories they did so with thirty thousand men, and the British government proposed to rule them with only twenty-two thousand men. The House should consider, he concluded, whether cutting troop strength might not end with the loss of all these new colonies to the crown and leave Britain merely a second-rate power. Then he argued a line that would define much of his life work as a politician. We should consider, he argued, "whether we should compel the crown to abandon all our colonial possessions, the fertile sources of our commercial wealth, and descend from that high and elevated station which had cost us so much labor, and much blood, and so much treasure to attain." British power abroad meant prestige, and prestige meant trade. To question this questioned the patriotic sacrifice of those who died to win the war against France.

As he began to speak out more in Parliament, Palmerston emerged as a younger man crossing into middle age, armed with some experience, exhibiting occasional flashes of startling good oratory and insight and a potential for future office. But this future seemed compromised by his reluctance to take on bigger tasks and by a lifestyle that gave an impression that dancing, fine wines, and making an appearance at Almack's epitomized his life ambition. As one early biographer of Palmerston stated, "No one went more into what is vulgarly termed 'fashionable society,' or attended more scrupulously to the affairs of his office." His constant round of dinners, plays, attention to racing, gambling, and to women defined his public image. He had certainly made an impact on British politics to date—but a small impact. Few would have predicted that he would soon represent a party and a rising class that would leave an indelible stamp not only on Britain but also on the makeup of the world.

3

Palmerston the Canningite

W hen Lord Liverpool died in 1827, the foreign secretary, George Canning, became prime minister. Canning served as foreign secretary from 1822 and continued the policy of his predecessor Lord Castlereagh in seeking a balance of power in Europe. But while seeking to maintain the balance of power, Canning gave up on "the Concert of Europe" that Castlereagh had utilized. The Concert of Europe brought together the heads of state, or representatives, of major European powers to work out political differences. This had worked well in settling affairs after the defeat of Napoleon. But Canning, even though a Tory, had liberal ideas that often contradicted the conservative monarchies that ruled Russia and Austria and, after the fall of Napoleon, France. Instead of reaching a consensus with governments who had ideas contrary to his own, Canning pursued a balance of power in Europe that sought to keep any one power from gaining preeminence and posing a threat to the liberties of Britain.

Palmerston's contemporaries considered him a "Canningite" because he supported the foreign policy of Canning. This policy differed from other conservative Tories because it often meant supporting liberal constitutional government over illiberal absolute monarchies. This policy began with Canning as foreign secretary under the prime minister, Lord Liverpool. Canning had previously served as foreign secretary under the Duke of Portland from 1807 to 1809. Canning's approach did not have the support of all, or even most, members of Parliament. Britain opposed revolutionary France in a long and bitter war and yet, as prime minister, Canning supported the revolutionary governments of Spanish Latin America against monarchical Spain. He also had peculiar influence in the formation of British informal empire in Latin America, a term scholars use to describe the extension of national power without the formal structures of empire. When the new Republics of Latin America declared their independence from Spain, the Spanish government—which had a great deal to lose if its colonies in Latin America could trade freely with other nations—asked Britain not to recognize them. But Canning persuaded the Liverpool administration to sign favorable free trade treaties with them—in effect recognizing them as independent states. Many members of Parliament vociferously objected—the monarchical Spanish government represented the very same government that had allied itself with Britain against their mutual enemy Napoleon. This act seemed to betray a friend and ally.

In 1822 Britain found itself in the peculiar position of pursuing a via media in foreign policy between the despotic monarchies on the continent and new revolutionary movements that shared much of the revolutionary enthusiasm that inspired the French Revolution and then the Napoleonic Wars. Canning, bucking the sentiments of many in his party, pressed to keep the monarchies of France, Prussia, Austria, and Russia from intervening to suppress revolution in Greece and Spain. When French troops invaded Spain to crush a popular revolt, Canning wisely understood that the British public—though they disapproved of the French actions—did not support another costly continental war. But when France threatened to aid the Monarchy of Spain in its attempt to reign in the new republics in Latin America, Canning drew the line. He made clear that Britain's navy would stop any transatlantic crossing of Spanish troops. The new republics would remain free from European dominance. To cement this action, he recognized three republics in 1825. "I resolved," he said, "that if France had Spain, it should not be Spain with the Indies. I called the new World into existence to redress the balance of the old." Canning insisted, and won free trade with Latin America. In doing so he set a precedent for Palmerston by using free trade in the region to lay the foundation for British power and prestige.

Other issues arose that challenged Canning's pledge to neutrality in the disputes between monarchies and revolution. The Greeks, suffering under the domination of the Ottoman empire, rose in a bloody revolt in the southern tip of the Greek peninsula, the Morea, killing thousands of the Turkish elite. The Turks responded with a brutal massacre at Smyrna, and the execution of the Greek Patriarch at Constantinople—a shockingly brutal act, equivalent in the Slavic world to the execution of the pope in Catholicism. Russia, a largely Slavic nation that often protected the interests of the Slavs in this region, moved south with an army.

In response, the Sultan, Mahmud II, enlisted the help of the autocratic modernizer of Egypt, Mehemet Ali, a powerful, despotic ruler who was still technically his vassal, and persuaded him to send an army into Greece to defend the Turks. This large navy and powerful army threatened mass destruction of the Greeks, and so Canning acted—responding to his own personal conscience on the issue and to public pressure. He allied Britain with Russia and France. His immediate successor in office, Viscount Goderich, ordered a combined fleet of Russian, British, and French ships to sink Mehemet's fleet at Navarino Bay in 1827. With this victory behind them, the allies negotiated with the Turks and won the autonomy of Greece.

Canning had shifted foreign policy from the neutrality of Castlereagh's to a policy that set the precedence for Palmerston throughout the mid-Victorian period. From this point on, with some exceptions, foreign policy favored constitutional government and free trade as the ruling principle between nations.

When, after the Napoleonic wars, Argentina, Columbia, Mexico, Venezuela, Honduras, and Brazil sought independence from monarchical Spain, Canning, with Palmerston in agreement, recognized the nations. This freed both the former Spanish colonies and Britain to pursue trade with each other at the expense of trade between the Spanish colonies and monarchical Spain. This radical step had powerful repercussions.

Canning, like Palmerston after him, held that free trade had the felicitous effect of improving the morals of the new trading countries. Palmerston later argued that "commerce is the best pioneer of civilization . . . [free trade joined] civilization with one hand, and peace with the other . . ." making men "happier, wiser, better." Free trade acted as a solvent against traditional landowning elites and gave money and power to the rising business class. The new merchant elite then demanded representative government. This led Canning to remark in 1824 that with trade and representative government, "South America is free and if we do not mismanage our affairs sadly, she is English." By this he meant that free trade led to better elites and to better government, and that in turn led to the world becoming far more like Britain, which, Canning and Palmerston were convinced, stood as a shining example of the most proper country on earth.

In April 1827, by then Prime Minister Canning offered the office of Chancellorship of the Exchequer to Palmerston. This time Palmerston agreed to accept a new office. But parliamentary rules for a cabinet level position required that he offer himself again for immediate reelection. But this strategy held definite risks; Canning and Palmerston agreed that he would remain at the war office until the next election, which would enable him to sweep into office with the rest of his party, and then take the position. But this tidy arrangement fell through. First, Palmerston had invested in a firm called the Devon Mining Company and sat on the board. When the company lost money, and many investors saw their funds go down the drain, the press reported the scandal and mentioned his name repeatedly. Secondly, the conflict with the king's brother over the Horse Guards earned him the enduring hostility of George IV, who did not want to see Palmerston act as the chief budget officer and treasurer of the government.

With these difficulties, Canning realized he had to withdraw the offer, and attempted to do so in a way that would not offend Palmerston. He asked him if he would be interested in being governor of Jamaica. "I laughed so heartily that I observed Canning looked quite put out, and I was obliged to grow serious again." Next, a few days later Canning offered him the governor-generalship of India. This he took seriously but also turned down, primarily because he wanted to stay close to the center, not the periphery of power. "That I felt what means it afforded for increasing one's fortune, for gratifying one's love for power, for affording a scope of doing good upon a magnificent theatre of action; but my ambition was satisfied with my position at home."

The Wellington Ministry

The Canning ministry did not last long, and Canning died August 8, 1827, having served only one hundred days as prime minister. After a short-lived government led by Viscount Goderich, the old war hero, the Duke of Wellington, formed his ministry and became the new prime minister. This put Palmerston in a strange position. As a Tory who leaned toward the Whigs not only politically but socially, he owed his election to Parliament to the fact that so many Whigs voted for him. Yet Wellington was a conservative Tory, and this meant that Palmerston felt obliged to him on a number of foreign policy issues.

As a "Canningite" he belonged to a small group of parliamentary members who saw their own political party in power but also saw their own party supporting illiberal governments overseas. Nonetheless, Wellington needed the support of the Canningites, and he included a number of them, including Palmerston, in his cabinet. At first this suited Palmerston fine, as long as the cabinet included others that shared his views—such as Lord Dudley at the Foreign Office. He knew serving with Wellington would disappoint the Whigs who hoped that Palmerston and other Canningites, by keeping distance from Wellington, would make a conservative ministry impossible. "The Whigs of course will be furious and violent, and lay about them to the right and left. I very sincerely regret their loss, as I like them much better than the Tories." Palmerston still held his old office of Secretary at War. He soon found himself, however, in bitter conflict with Tory policies, and this conflict paved the way for his final break with the Tories and his crossing over the aisle to the Whigs. He lasted in the Wellington ministry only five months.

Palmerston and Wellington differed on many issues: on Russia, the Ottoman empire, the Greek rebellion, and constitutional government in Portugal. These disagreements give a preview to Palmerston's approach on foreign policy that would define much of his agenda as foreign secretary, and then prime minister. Wellington feared the Russians and feared war. Palmerston feared the loss of constitutional liberty, and the instability of radical French Revolution–style politics. But he wanted reform and progress by small steps. To a modern, this may sound like a slight difference, but Palmerston's approach proved feasible: he desired alteration by degrees that enabled the world to change radically over time without revolution.

Wellington also worried about a general European war erupting from Russian advances. When the Russians surrounded Constantinople in 1829 and extracted the treaty of Adrianople from the Ottoman government, they gained colonies on the shore of the Black Sea, shipping rights through the straights of Dardanelles, and Moldavia and Walachia. Wellington saw them moving south, and west, but he managed to use diplomacy to draw the map of Greece in 1830 right before his government fell. Britain, along with much of the continent, prized ancient Greek literature and romanticized democratic Athens. The modern Greeks also professed Christianity, so opinion tended to side with the Greeks against the Turks. Lord Byron, immensely popular as a poet, sailed to Greece and died for the cause of democracy and Greek nationalism. In spite of these considerations, Wellington wanted no more trouble from Greece and did not support the independence movement there.

While Wellington's ministry struggled with these issues, Palmerston had taken a harsh line. No longer in the Wellington cabinet, he gave speeches in Parliament that indicated to some that he angled for a future position as foreign secretary. He lambasted the government on how it handled Greece and mocked the idea of drawing boundaries so small that Greece "should contain neither Athens, nor Thebes, nor Marathon, nor Salamis, nor Platea, nor Thermopylae, nor Missolonoghi, which should exclude from its boundaries all the most inspiring records of national achievements, whether in ancient or modern times."

Another issue arose that gave Palmerston the chance to distance himself from the Wellington administration. When Miguel, younger son of the late King John of Portugal, overthrew the constitutional government of Portugal and instituted absolutism, Wellington chose noninterference, taking a particularly Castlereagh-like line against the liberal interference of Canning, who preceded him. Palmerston erupted in outrage, "The civilized world rings with excretions upon Miguel; and yet this destroyer of constitutional freedom, this breaker of solemn oaths, this faithless usurper , this enslaver of his country . . . [is] not sufficiently refuted by any acts of the British Government."

Palmerston argued for interference close to home, in Portugal, that characterized his interference with large swaths of the world before his career ended,

> If by "interference" is meant interference by force of arms, such interference, the Government are right in saying, "general principals and our own practice forbade us to exert." But if by "interference" is meant intermeddling, and intermeddling in every way, and to every extent, short of actual military force; then I must affirm, that there is nothing in such interference, which the law of nations may not in certain cases permit.

When King George IV died, the great opponent to Palmerston holding prominent office lay in the grave. Wellington after new elections tried to form another government, and Palmerston knew the time had come to cross the aisle and support the Whigs. Palmerston appealed to the strengths of both parties. A slow reformer at home, this pleased a cautious landed elite. He pushed hard for interference abroad that would lead to a world that would look much more like England than absolutist Russia, and this pleased the rising middle and business classes. His language shows his complete dedication to republican ideals. When constitutional government triumphed in Portugal he exulted, "We shall drink to the cause of Liberalism all over the world. . . . This event is decisive of the ascendancy of Liberal Principals throughout Europe; the evil spirit has been put down and will be trodden under foot. . . ."

The Ministry of Lord Grey

Lord Grey, a Whig, entered office as prime minister, and on November 19, 1830, he tendered the Foreign Office to Palmerston. This time Palmerston offered no refusal, and the world at large was about to feel his imprint. After the Congress of Vienna in 1815, diplomats expected Britain to take a leading part in world affairs and often to act as the arbiter of disputes. The British, backed by the largest economy in the world and a navy that could sweep clear the seas of any region of the world, felt the responsibility keenly. Some critics would argue too keenly, with John Bull acting as a type of stern father, settling disputes between unruly children and inflicting punishment when necessary. Liberal opinion felt that the foreign secretary should use his office to advance universal principles such as free trade, democracy, and evenhandedness between nations. Liberal opinion also expected Realpolitiks—practical action that included the hardheaded use of military force—to judiciously make the bullies of the world step into line and to advance the obviously superior Christian European civilization. Palmerston, entering office, never doubted what the public wanted of him and played—sincerely—to the gallery of newspaper-reading spectators at home.

With a confidence that few in Parliament possessed, Palmerston calmly strode across the parliamentary floor and took his place next to Lord Grey as a new member of his Whig-dominated cabinet. At this party time affiliation vacillated, quite unlike membership in a club—and it depended upon perception. Party affiliation meant that a Member of Parliament came to office on the votes of those who tended toward Tory or Whig policies. So when Palmerston crossed the aisle to associate with the Whigs and other liberal Tories who served in a Whig administration, this new affiliation began to crystallize in the mind of the public. When the Tories defeated Palmerston in an 1831 election at Cambridge University, Palmerston subsequently sought election in a Whig-dominated countrywide election at Blechingley. There the electors returned him promptly and impressed on the public his new status as a Whig. As a Canningite he had already flirted with Whig positions—after all he supported free trade and supported Catholic emancipation. Therefore his crossing to the other side of the aisle astonished but did not shock the members of Parliament.

Not only men watched his progress in politics. Two women in particular played a large role in his life and may have shaped some of his policies. Persistent rumor linked Palmerston to Madame Lieven, wife of the Russian ambassador. Gossipers in society simply assumed that they had an affair and that this affair explained his pro-Russian views. The evidence shows only friendship, though the common perception may accurately describe the relationship and its influence. Originally from Latvia and of German heritage, Madame Lieven grew up in the court of Czar Paul I and was married at a young age to Count Lieven. When she arrived at the court of St. James she benefited in society from the war with Napoleon, which gave her entrée into fashionable circles. Northwestern Europeans considered Russia a crude, backward, threatening backwater at the time, but because Russia joined Britain as an ally against the French, Madame Lieven enjoyed fashionable status. She even found her way into the exclusive Almack's club and socialized there with Palmerston and at other aristocratic dinners and dances. If she did have an affair with Palmerston it would complete an impressive triangle of influence, for she also had affairs with Prince von Metternich, the long-serving foreign minister of the Austrian empire, and Francois Guizot, the French foreign minister.

She wrote often to the empress dowager, the mother of the czar, and to her own brother in Russia, about life in England, politics, scandal, and the cabinet, gleaning much information from her contacts, including Palmerston. To her Russian correspondents she referred to Palmerston as "our minister," because of his pro-Russian bias in the 1830s. She certainly bragged that her influence secured him the position of foreign secretary by her intervention with Lord Grey. But Palmerston did not repay the favor. They quarreled, particularly over his appointment of an ambassador to the Russian court that she—and her emperor—disapproved of. After the quarrel he arranged the recall of the Russian ambassador to Britain, and this meant of course that his wife, Madame Lieven, who had lived in London for over twenty years, also had to leave. She bitterly resented it. She had a habit of discussing her friends behind their backs and giving away state secrets to her correspondents, and so her departure from society left behind few who regretted the action, the Duke of Wellington remarking that she had done "this country all the mischief in her power in return for much kindness and good will."

Another woman in Palmerston's life, however, retained his affections permanently. Emily Lamb, daughter of his mentor Lord Melbourne, moved gracefully through society, "like a pale flower" in the words of her brother, and seemed to leave a trail of society men in love with her deep voice and beautiful languid eyes. Palmerston knew her for thirty years before they married. She was Lady Cowper, one of the patronesses at Almack's. There she sat on the board and admitted into the club only the socially acceptable and those she liked. An applicant from the middle class, for instance, who had made a fortune in manufacturing, rarely made it in. The patronesses even turned down aristocrats if thought cross or boring. Palmerston, regarded as a pleasing conversation partner with women, instantly gained access on application and there met Lady Cowper.

They had a long-standing affair before they married, because though Palmerston loved her very much she had at the age of eighteen married Earl Cowper during the war years. Earl Cowper let her move freely in society, and he did not question her friendships with other men. He point-blank refused to fight duels to protect her name from insult because, as he once remarked, half the men in London offered challenges. Softhearted and kind, she cared intimately for the poor on her estate, unable to deny a request for help. Nor, vicious gossipers added, did she deny high-ranking men making passionate demands. We do know that though Palmerston and Lady Cowper had friendships, and possibly affairs with others, they held each other in constant affection.

Palmerston asked her to marry him after the death of Earl Cowper, and he went on asking for a number of years. Emily Cowper's brother, Lord Melbourne, now also prime minister, advised caution. Palmerston, he felt, may not have had much money to live on outside of the income from his office. He also had many debts, lived in high style, and had launched many projects of improvement on his estates in Ireland (such as building schools, roads, and a port) that brought in few profits. When they finally became engaged young Queen Victoria giggled at the idea of an older couple getting married. The queen had married in 1839 her own young husband, Albert, with whom she fell deeply in love. With Palmerston at fifty-five and Emily Lamb (Lady Cowper) at fifty-two years of age she wondered why they bothered to marry so late.

But the marriage proved very successful. Lady Cowper thought her new title—Lady Palmerston—had a nice ring to it. She loved Broadlands, situated on the edge of New Forest with a prominent stream meandering across the estate visible from her favorite room. She loved the treasures collected from all over Europe by the late Viscount Palmerston. If the marriage settled "Lord Cupid" down—and it did, somewhat—it also solidified and extended his influence in politics. She soon became a favorite hostess—particularly for their house in London in Carlton Terrace, No. 5, near Hyde Park. She visited often with Queen Victoria, and her daughters from her former marriage made the court their second home; one served as Lady of the Bedchamber, a formal title that really meant, in this case, "young friend to the young queen." Lady Palmerston's parties solidified her husband's standing with the sovereign and made him look less of a gadfly and more substantial, a serious man with weight and standing.

Foreign Secretary

While Palmerston had the reputation of a playboy in society, he worked hard to demonstrate the opposite. At the Foreign Office he discouraged play. He banned smoking by the clerks in "the nursery," the main office where the clerks in the Foreign Office worked. He put an end to clerks' catcalling at female garment workers seen through the windows of another building. Clerks worked late into the night, until ten o'clock, and quite often on Sunday. These clerks came from aristocratic families and expected interesting and amusing work. For the most part they copied and filed letters. This means that clerks made records of instructions to ambassadors, agents, and other officials overseas, and also copies of their responses. They corrected documents; they created abstracts or condensed versions of information that came in daily to the office for the perusal of Palmerston. They ate many meals in the office with little time to go home and have a proper dinner. Married men often complained of the state of affairs under Palmerston. Some clerks stayed in the position for a career, but most moved on, many of them running for Parliament. So when Palmerston moved from the War Office to the Foreign Office, taking with him his hard-driving work ethic, he did not endear himself among the workers. The clerks nicknamed him "Protocol Palmerston."

But if the clerks did not generally like Palmerston they did respect him. He worked harder than any foreign secretary in memory, having once told Queen Victoria that he drafted all the dispatches and instructions personally because the European practice of handing responsibilities to subordinates gave the foreign secretaries less mastery of detail and less control over events. He needed all the control he could muster, for his first duties as foreign secretary involved decisions that could easily plunge Europe into war if not handled with discretion.

As soon as he came into office another revolution broke out in France. He had already foreseen the revolution coming under the very conservative King Charles X, who "learned nothing and forgot nothing." Charles raised taxes to pay compensation to nobles returning to France from exile, he strengthened the laws against sacrilege, and attempted to reintroduce the right of primogeniture, by which the oldest son inherited all the land, and which served as the cornerstone for large landed estates. The middle classes would have none of it, and brought in Louis Philippe as their new king. The British public, alarmed at the prospect of another French Revolution, soon applauded the ascent of a new monarch dedicated to the idea of a constitutional monarchy that reflected British sentiments.

This was a revolution Palmerston liked very much because it differed so radically from the previous revolution of 1789. The French Revolution of 1830 looked far more like the British "Glorious Revolution" of 1688 because the Parisian middle class that led the fighting accomplished their goal in only three days with limited bloodshed, and because the aristocratic and middle class agreed to the moderate, dispassionate King Louis Philippe. On the surface the resulting arrangement resembled the constitutional system of checks and balances much inspired by the British example. Liberty without extremis or, as Palmerston boasted, happy with the spread of British-inspired ideas of governance, "We shall drink the cause of liberalism all over the world. Let Spain and Austria look to themselves; this reaction cannot end where it began and Spain and Italy and Portugal and parts of Germany will sooner or later be affected. This event is decisive of the ascendancy of Liberal Principles throughout Europe."

But the revolution had wheels and soon careened off of its French track and crashed into the carefully constructed political entity called the United Kingdom of the Netherlands. Holland and Belgium had been in 1814 merged into a single country with the express purpose, under British direction, of protecting Belgium from future French aggression. But William of Orange, the reigning monarch of the Netherlands, could not successfully fuse the two cultures of Belgium and Holland into one entity. On August 25, 1830, after an opera closed in Brussels, the patrons spilled onto the streets in a rebellious and exuberant mood, inspired by the performance of *La Muette de Portici,* which portrayed Italian city republics in rebellion. The republican rebellion in France also clearly inspired the Brussels audience, which, already giddy from the fine performance, began to riot in the streets. Other parts of Belgium took up the fight, and soon the Dutch retreated in a confused rout. All Europe watched in horror. The Concert of Europe that had worked so well to secure the peace dissolved before the public gaze, and another devastating European-wide war, with republican governments overthrowing church and throne, threatened once again to burn elegant cities to the ground, raze the mansions of the old landed elites, and send the traditional rulers of Europe, who considered themselves so cultivated and judicious, packing as refugees fleeing the mob.

At this point, Palmerston called a meeting of the ambassadors of leading powers to London for a conference. If one thinks of the meeting as a card game with much of the world watching, Palmerston sat down at the negotiating table with a strong hand. First, he hosted the conference in London. Britain had played the leading diplomatic role since the end of the Napoleonic wars. But additionally, Palmerston knew the French language and culture well from his many visits to Paris. He rightly guessed that while the French wanted the expansion of republicanism, they did not want a major war. Never officially discussed, but understood, the devastating power of the navy backed Britain up at the negotiating table and gave Palmerston the power to enforce a blockade at sea and crush France economically. Britain could also use the occasion of a blockade to strip away more French colonies. So he entered the conference with a clear idea of how far France would push its desire to expand republican government and when France would give up. Pragmatism, not idealism, ruled his judgment. He saw that if the Belgians did not want Holland to rule them and if Britain wanted to keep Belgium from turning to France for help, then he had no choice but to buttress the claims for independence. The agreement hinged on reaching consensus on the species of monarchy acceptable to all the major powers sitting around the table.

Louis-Philippe also helped Palmerston craft a successful solution. The French king could have sent an expansionist general as ambassador but sent instead the aging Talleyrand, who had served the French since the revolution and wanted peace in Europe. Both Palmerston and Talleyrand declared their intentions to settle the issue fairly, and both saw much in common with each other, though they had been ancient foes: both rejected the divine right of kings as a doctrine, unlike the monarchies of Prussia, Austria, and Russia, and both had a constitutional form of government that gave some voice to the middle classes.

Palmerston crafted his early reputation in diplomacy by gingerly handling Belgium, dubbed by the press the "cock-pit of Europe," and inverting a crisis into triumph. Few diplomats could unravel this Gordian knot. Louis-Philippe had the expansionist republican left, concentrated in Paris, boiling over with republican enthusiasm, craving to restore Belgium as part of France. Prussia and allied German states would never have tolerated French possession of Belgium. The Dutch king William of Orange wanted Belgium back in his control. The British saw the old Concert of Europe falling apart and a general war looming. Pouring fuel on the fire, the French army then marched into Brussels, with little opposition, and took possession.

Palmerston responded by choreographic steps of diplomacy, getting the other major powers, Russia, Prussia, the Netherlands, along with Britain, to bring pressure to bear on France. Palmerston wrote, "One thing is certain, the French must go out of Belgium, or we have general war, and a war in a given number of days." This he said in a letter he knew the French secret police would intercept. He played his hand well, for the French agreed to give up Belgium. But the Belgians and the Dutch fumed at the territorial concessions—the Belgians gained so little and the Dutch lost so much. The prime minister, Lord Grey, remarked irritably, "What is to be done with these damned Dutch and Belgians?" Nothing seemed to satisfy them. But Palmerston even succeeded in bringing the French to cooperate actively. By working together, the French with troops on the ground and the British blockading the approach to Belgium by sea, they forged a settlement, one could say forced a settlement. Belgium received independence, and the French left the country. Belgium agreed to tear down a number of fortifications built by the former allies to protect Europe from French aggression—a bone thrown to republicans in France. General war was averted, France kept in her place, and a constitutional monarchy established with the unobjectionable Prince Leopold of Saxe-Coburg on the throne (becoming Leopold I of Belgium).

Palmerston's stock at home and abroad soared at these unexpected triumphs. In hindsight, historians have seen darker clouds on the horizon of the settlement. After all, Castlereagh had earlier arranged a European-wide system that guaranteed the peace of Europe, and Palmerston failed to keep the "concert" in place. He rewarded rioters with independence—this only encouraged revolution elsewhere. In addition, keeping Belgium out of France weakened the French and perhaps invited future conflicts with Germany in 1867 and 1914. But such speculation proceeds on very thin and unconvincing evidence. Palmerston often supported revolution abroad and often supported those that helped remake the world into an English image with a constitutional government, a free press, free trade, and freedom of religion. The Belgium affair gave a foretaste of things to come.

Reform

Even at a relatively early point of his career Palmerston began to have doubts about his party affiliation. While his defense of a strong military endeared him to the other Tories, his sympathies with limited electoral reform revealed that he was flirting shamelessly with the Whigs. While most of the members of Parliament, even the large landowners, realized that public opinion demanded reform of some description, they did not agree among themselves on the shape and substance of the reform needed. Each party, Whig and Tory, had members that disagreed violently with each other. They agreed on some points, however, and that explains how Palmerston had a foot in each camp.

Palmerston, similarly with most Tories and Whigs, found the electoral system confusing and outdated. The current system provided a fair representation of the counties. Each county sent two members, much like each state in the United States sends two senators to the Senate, regardless of the size of the state's population. (York County sent four, because of its larger population—the sole exception). Although both parties practiced bribery, politicians found it harder to corrupt the elections in the countryside. With large populations spread thinly over extensive territories, candidates strained to organize and pay off voters.

But members of Parliament agreed that the boroughs cried out for reform. The boroughs were cities or towns that sent members to Parliament. Corruption defined them for a number of reasons. First, the crown appointed the boroughs for representation in the Middle Ages and early modern period. Many of these "cities" dwindled in size and even disappeared altogether. So the local landlord used his influence with a handful of electors, often his tenants, to "pocket" the vote, that is, choose the Member of Parliament as he wished. Other areas had grown to large cities like Leeds and Manchester, and returned not a single member to Parliament. The boroughs had no single standard of who qualified to vote, and sometimes a handful of electors determined the election. The "owners" of boroughs (the local landlord usually, though in a few cases the treasury controlled the borough) sold their vote to the highest bidder. Or, often the case, candidates canvassed the electors with promises, free food, liquor, and often, outside payments of cash. Finally, most members understood the need to give some representation to the massive cities springing up in the industrial north of England that had no representation in Parliament at all.

But beyond this simple agreement for some reform, the disagreements multiplied. The moderates wished no more than to eliminate the boroughs that embarrassed the nation with gross corruption and to leave the rest intact. Others, inspired by the ideals of the French Revolution, demanded a complete overhaul with equal representation for every male that paid taxes. While the logic of reform corresponds to many political ideas today, many members of Parliament advanced arguments against reform that held great sway with their fellow countrymen and had a peculiar and powerful logic of their own. First, many of the most talented members, indeed most, in the nineteenth century, came into power through a corrupt borough. How could this be good? Because Whigs and Tories (later liberals and conservatives) needed talented youth to enter their ranks. When such a youth shone at Oxford or Cambridge (or elsewhere) the elders of the party took notice and often sponsored them into Parliament through a rotten borough before the youth had built up a broad base of political support. This led to a steady stream of clear-thinking youths with good oratorical skills entering Parliament and benefiting the country with their talent. In addition, experienced elder statesmen, after losing a local election, often returned to the Parliament by another borough. This saved many valuable party leaders and experienced veterans for service to their country. "Corruption" guaranteed that talent, new and old, flowed in a steady stream to Parliament. Other reasons against reform ring hollow today, such as the contention that the landed elite were entitled to office. This latter argument however held great sway in Palmerston's time.

Palmerston remembered the day the Reform Act of 1832 passed, for the rest of his life. The issue had long been debated and sharply divided political opinion. The historian and parliamentarian Thomas Macaulay has dramatically told the story of its passage, the broad outline of which follows. On the day that the final vote for reform arrived, the crowd overflowed the House of Commons. More legislators packed into the chamber than at any time in memory—608 members present. When the last debate had ended and the speaker called for the vote it sounded like two broadsides of cannon—aye, one side shouted; nay, the other. Unable to discern the winner, the House resorted to counting—not by raising hands but by separation. The no votes stood, and walked into the lobby to take roll. It seemed an army of legislators had risen and left the chamber. The supporters of reform looked around in alarm. So many had left, surely they lost the vote. The rule of landlords would not end. The whole country would rise in the streets and riot, they feared.

Those who remained counted their numbers nervously. Tellers moved row-by-row, ticking off the bodies. 290, 296, 299, with 300 came a gasp. Was that enough to win? 302. No more. How many did the opposition have? Then the doors to the lobby flew open and the legislators against reform came pouring into the room talking wildly as they came. Disorder reigned, no one seemed in charge. Rumors of numbers flew. How many in opposition? There were 303 of them, no, 310, and 307. Finally Charles Wood, who took the count of the no votes in the lobby jumped on a bench and his voice boomed over the crowd: "They are only three hundred and one!" Thomas Macaulay wrote, "We set up a shout that you might have heard to Charing Cross, waving our hats, stamping against the floor, and clapping our hands."

Many legislators shed tears. The leader of the opposition, Peel, sat with jaw open, unbelieving. A crowd from the House moved toward the doors, which swung open and into the lobby. From there the crowd of thousands of onlookers, packed in the lobby, in the stairways, and outside surrounding Parliament, let out a shout that moved like a gigantic wave from the lobby, down the stairs, and out into the surrounding crowd. The reforming legislators forced their way out of the building, waving their hats. Reform had passed at last.

What did the Reform Act of 1832 accomplish? It accelerated the shift from the rule of landlords to the upper middle class. The aristocracy still played a leading role in society, and would continue to do so for many decades. But from this time forward they lacked the same power once reserved exclusively to them. Nonetheless they still held great influence and continued to represent in Parliament and in government office the power of the ruling middle and upper middle class. After this vote Britain, the economic engine of the world, roared ahead at full speed and became a great agent of globalization and reform.

The Limits of Power

While Palmerston had substantial power as foreign secretary, he also faced serious limitations. He worked with a small staff. In 1841, for instance, he supervised twenty-four clerks, with eight other employees. In 1849 the foreign office received thirty thousand incoming dispatches—some small and quickly dealt with, others long and complex. Palmerston and his staff spent most of their time reading and writing, usually late into the night. He once commented to the queen that all this work gave the foreign secretary an advantage because, when the time came for the Foreign Office to defend itself before Parliament, the office staff knew their business intimately.

The size of the navy and the army, and the paucity of money also limited Palmerston's options. Britain relied heavily on naval supremacy for influence around the world, and even those like member of Parliament William Cobbett, who campaigned hard for free trade and often spoke wistfully of a world without empires, supported the navy, which he described as "our bulwark." The press too, generally, supported strong spending on naval forces. But while the navy gave many options for interference abroad, the army limited this interference. Britain based its power on the open seas and tried to avoid continental wars after 1815. Because of the sheer size of the British empire and its impact in the world, it seems logical that Britain should have a very large army. But except for the two hundred thousand–strong Indian army under the East India Company, Britain held a comparatively small standing army at home. When Palmerston became foreign secretary Britain had an army of sixty-four thousand soldiers. This fact explains many of the fears Britain had about large land powers—the queen often expressed alarm on this score. The Prussian army, unifying the German states, terrified the British, as did the Russian army with its huge troop reserves. A large land war drained money from an expanding economy, increased taxes, and meant hiring an army of bureaucrats to oversee the war. A strong navy guaranteed isolation from the continent—and thus war—allowing Britain to look overseas for expansion.

Within the limits of his power Palmerston used the Foreign Office to open markets. Trade supplied the lifeline of Britain, and most of this trade occurred outside of Europe. While continental European governments also had free trade, and while the Industrial Revolution slowly seeped into northwestern Europe throughout the nineteenth century, governments supervised and limited economic activities in Europe to an extent that the British found unjustifiable. Britain pursued open markets around the world, what the philosopher Thomas Carlyle called the "cash nexus," that is, a rule of law that protected property and contracts, and a trade policy that opened resources to all capitalists on an equal footing. Britain pursued these policies, draped in humanitarian concerns that promoted modernization, civilization, and mutual benefit. Diplomats used force as an option to police regions that resisted open trade with Britain.

Palmerston did not hesitate to go to war for the right conditions, and he used the navy for this purpose liberally. He rarely used force in Europe, though among the weaker states of Spain, Portugal, Greece, and Naples he did intervene to enforce constitutional rule. He intervened often outside of Europe—in Africa, China, the Middle East, and Latin America. Palmerston justified the use of force as part of the civilizing mission, and necessary for opening markets, or in his words, "world bettering." He felt that "half-civilized governments" required "a dressing every eight to ten years to keep them in order." Implied in Palmerston's use of the word is a "dressing down" or a beating, much in the manner that a Victorian parent disciplined unruly children. This chauvinist doctrine proved handy for it gave the British government leeway to support any movement of self-determination in its interest, while allowing Britain to withhold support from any government or movement that did not fit its interest. To aid or oppose revolution gave Britain one tool among many to shape its growing informal empire.

Exuberance and mere surfeit of ambition did not lead Palmerston to bully foreign powers. Fears drove many of his actions, fears that had solid ground in recent European history. He worried that extremist elements abroad conspired to destroy the British way of life, which included constitutional government. Constitutional government represented to Palmerston hope for the whole of humanity—all elements of a society worked together, the aristocracy, merchants, working men, compromising to make a civil and advanced society possible. If one class triumphed, then the other strata of society disintegrated and liberty disappeared. If the aristocracy alone triumphed, then absolutism, as with the despot monarchies on the continent in Russia, Prussia, and Austria, prevailed—leaving the country economically backward, dangerously expansionist, with intellectual culture languishing. If the middle classes prevailed, then, as happened in the French Revolution under Robespierre and Napoleon, tyranny triumphed.

In Europe, Palmerston had to balance the Holy Alliance against the radicals who supported wholesale democratic reform. Russia, Austria, and Prussia, dedicated to the support of traditional monarchies and Christian faith, formed the Holy Alliance as a response to revolutionary pressure. They represented a fundamentalism of ideas and a pan-European commitment of antirevolutionary strategy that was quite alien to the eighteenth-century Palmerstonian style of diplomacy that emphasized self-interest and pragmatism. Also, the Holy Alliance had to fight against radical revolution, and thus came to resemble its own enemies in its strident tone and feverish opposition to revolution.

Outside of Europe Palmerston had to contend with the United States as another world power. He tolerated the United States as an unstable democracy—unpredictable, expansionist, and lusting after Latin America, perhaps even parts of Asia. Palmerston felt that Americans used culture as a mere veneer over crass materialism. Culture never took deep root because Americans lacked the balancing factor of a refined aristocratic class. Against these extremes of the left and right, Palmerston saw himself as ringmaster in an international arena, using the superior British navy and economy to maintain the safety of the high seas and the openness of markets. He nudged governments abroad toward the middle ground of constitutional rule. If he failed, he feared for the extinction of liberty for not only Britain but for the whole world.

Revolutions of 1848

The greatest test of Palmerston's tenure in the Foreign Office came in 1848. The European revolutions of 1848 swept monarchs off their thrones and threatened the old order across central and Western Europe and surprised almost everyone. Palmerston, though, seemed nonplussed and seemed to stand alone among prominent statesmen by keeping an evenhanded and calm outlook. The wave of revolutions first hit France and forced its monarch Louis Philippe to flee to England. Metternich, the foreign secretary of Austria and longtime adversary of Palmerston, fled by night from Vienna on March 15 as the riots in the street spread to government buildings. Terrified, Metternich exclaimed, "After me the deluge." The emperor Ferdinand of the Austro-Hungarian empire swiftly offered to appease the middle-class revolutionaries with a new constitution, one for Hungary, and one for Austria. William IV of Prussia swiftly followed with a liberal constitution. Smaller principalities in central Europe followed suit. The old regime abandoned the palace and ran for its life. In Britain alarm ran high.

The Chartist demonstrations in Britain echoed the revolution in Europe. Chartists had their roots in the late-eighteenth-century reaction against the Industrial Revolution and in the radical politics that animated the revolutions in Europe, emphasizing the belief in universal suffrage for all males. But the Chartists lacked the stabilizing force of the middle class. In Britain, the compromising political arrangements of the 1688 constitution and the reform undertaken by Parliament in 1832 wooed the middle class into cooperation. This however, left behind artisans, radical reformers, and a variety of individuals who felt displaced by the market forces that disrupted the traditional relationship to the land, to village life, community, and meaningful (nonfactory) employment.

The last great demonstration of Chartists occurred in 1848 on Kennington Common, London. With monarchies tumbling in Europe, many British worried that revolution would sweep their own country as well. But cool heads prevailed at Whitehall, and the demonstration, carefully guarded with four thousand policemen, thousands more troops, and thousands of volunteers, ended peacefully. The Chartists presented a petition to Parliament, which promptly rejected it. The movement, bereft of the strength of the growing middle class, which preferred the established order and slow reform, slowly dissolved. "A glorious day" Palmerston declared, when the Chartist demonstration came to nothing.

In Europe, the tidal wave of revolution also largely dissipated, the deluge, as Metternich called it, slowly draining away. Compromise combined with firm action cleared the revolutionaries out of Vienna, Berlin, and Frankfurt. France declined to march into adjacent countries and force revolution, as happened with Napoleon. Austria maintained her grip of the possessions she held on the Italian peninsula. While Queen Victoria felt alarm at the proceedings in Europe, Palmerston rightly judged the situation and did not overreact. He formally recognized any form of government that came into power during these affairs— a very practical move. He distinguished between treaty obligations and a guarantee, a perhaps deceptive verbal play, but one he could use to keep Britain out of a continental war when he chose. He wrote that "the fact of having been one of the signatory powers of such a treaty gives the right to intervene, but does not impose on it the obligation to do so, in the case in which the state possession has been changed." That is, if a new government has come to power, Britain is not obliged to keep to the treaty, unless a guarantee has been made. This doctrine came in handy when Nicholas I, czar of Russia, sent troops into Hungary and other areas in central Europe to crush revolution. Palmerston had no intention of being drawn into a European war because of Russia's power play in her own backyard. Palmerston wrote shrewdly, "Much as Her Majesty's Government regret this interference of Russia, the causes which have led to it, and the effects which it may produce, they nevertheless have not considered the occasion to be one which at present calls for any formal expression of the opinions of Great Britain on the matter."

Palmerston laid down a flexible doctrine that enabled Britain to support regimes friendly to British influence and to oppose others. In the turmoil on the continent over Italian independence, he opposed the censures of the king of Sardinia and the annexations that laid the foundation for Italian unity put forth by other European powers. Later, as prime minister, Palmerston's Secretary of State, John Russell, stated in a dispatch to the European powers that "when a people from good reasons take up arms against an oppressor, it is but an act of justice and generosity to assist brave men in the defense of their liberties. . . . Her Majesty's Government will turn their eyes . . . to the gratifying prospect of a people building up the edifice of their liberties, and consolidating the work of their independence. . . ." These sentiments were rarely applied to central Europe and the United States, where Britain had less power. Palmerston chose to see the revolutions of 1848 as nationalism and not radicalism. In addition he may have felt a little cleaning house of old, creaky, autocratic regimes would do some good. He proceeded cautiously, however, knowing the devastation of a European-wide war. He has been credited with accomplishing much in this crisis by doing little—that is by not overreacting. In the rest of the world, he did not tiptoe quite so diplomatically.

The case of the 1848 revolutions show that Palmerston seemed to lead Britain in an independent direction from the other states of Europe. His manner, not merely his politics, illustrates this. He had in his style of leadership something breezy, easygoing, and quick to act, to fight, and to force open doors. But the peculiarities of his personality do not explain it all. Much of this style grew from his early influences and from his age, which enabled him to look back to an earlier century. His mentor, Lord Malmesbury, had coached him from his youth in the style of eighteenth-century diplomacy. Malmesbury served Britain in the court of King Frederick in Prussia, and then Catherine of Russia, in an age when alliances shifted easily and few fundamental precepts guided diplomacy. Neither ideas, ideology, nor high-sounding principles moved the diplomats of the eighteenth century like Malmesbury, but rather contingency, and a polite, mannered pursuit of national interest. What seemed so modern about Palmerston in resisting the Holy Alliance and pursuing free trade, liberalism, and English national interest actually derived from the eighteenth century and lived in his own memory of his father and his old mentor, Lord Malmesbury. It also placed him squarely in the tradition of his predecessor, Canning, who, first and foremost a patriot, never let strong principles interfere with the best interest of Britain. Palmerston at times sounded like a revolutionary, at times an aristocratic autocrat. But at all times he pursued British interest first and sailed his ship of state sometimes into war, sometimes into peaceful harbors, but almost always to victory and to power with an almost uncanny ability to read the sentiment of the British public that gave him an authority overseas unmatched by any other foreign secretary.

Palmerston had boundless physical energy and a popularity with the electorate based on his air of casualness, a happy-go-lucky temperament. Highly intelligent, he nonetheless possessed a mind fitted with, as one biographer, Lord Cecil, phrased it, "a clearness sufficient but not too great [for] the House of Commons." He also brought with him an approach to other diplomats that almost wrecked the negotiating proceedings again and again, a direct style lacking courtly manners or refinement—many diplomats saw him as rude and overbearing.

Palmerston succeeded in spite of these detriments because he represented a new type of politician, one whose power lay far less with an aristocratic web of cooperation than with the press. Newspapers tended to have their loyalties toward either the Whigs or the Tories, and Palmerston counted on the loyalty of the Whig papers. Political party money paid for the publication and support of numerous papers to publish the party line, and Palmerston relied heavily on these papers to get across to the public his own point of view.

But behind his jaunty image lurked fear. While Britain took the lead in the Industrial Revolution, other countries showed signs of industrial might. While the British economy continued to grow, the economies in other northwest European countries, particularly in Prussia and the German states, grew more, year by year. The United States also loomed as a future industrial giant. This meant a number of things for the future, but the availability of markets loomed as the most pressing issue. New trading partners would feed the roaring fire that fueled the steam engine of British strength. This need for markets drove Palmerston to interfere abroad and lay behind his push for free trade and informal empire.

Informal Empire and Free Trade

The struggle for global influence did not always involve the larger powers. The "Belgium affair," for instance, revealed Palmerston's deeply held assumptions and gave a clue to the kind of protocols that he would employ in the future in many parts of the globe: (1) the British fleet backed up diplomacy, (2) diplomacy supported British interest, and (3) British interest lay in supporting states that practiced free trade and did not bend the knee to other great powers. We also see that Palmerston considered war inevitable and nothing to avoid when needed, unless war led to a European-wide conflict. These principles generally guided Palmerston for the rest of his tenure in office, both as foreign secretary and as prime minister. While Gladstone, often supported the use of force reluctantly, we nonetheless see these Palmerstonian principles followed by Disraeli and Salisbury, two prominent prime ministers in the latter part of the nineteenth century.

The specific challenges that lay ahead in one region after another enabled him to use these principles and place his stamp on much of the formal and informal empire. It should be kept in mind that neither Palmerston nor other mid-Victorian officials used the term "informal empire." Rather they thought in terms of an empire of trade. They envisioned an influence that would transform regions of the world into the image of England. Free trade gave more income to the business class, who then demanded more say in government, leading often to pressure for a constitutional form of government not unlike England's. Civilization also followed the wake of trade. Palmerston felt that "commerce is the best pioneer of civilization . . . [free trade joined] civilization with one hand and peace with the other . . ." making men "happier, wiser, better." Most importantly, free trade challenged the traditional landowning elites of "backward nations" and allowed a new set of people to take over the reins of these societies. When the merchant class gained more money from trade it took over control of government, slowly displacing the old landed elites. Trade meant change, civilization, and republican forms of government. As George Canning had remarked in 1824, supremely confident of the benefits of trade, "South America is free and if we do not mismanage our affairs sadly, she is English."

Palmerston often sparred in Parliament with Richard Cobden, who played such a vital role in the abolition of the Corn Laws. But much as they disagreed—particularly about the need for a growing empire—they shared many assumptions. Though Cobden objected to Palmerston's use of force to spread British ideals, they shared the utopian vision that free trade created a radically different and better world. Cobden wrote:

> [Free trade involved a] principle that . . . will act on the moral world as the principle of gravitation in the universe,—drawing men together, thrusting aside the antagonism of race, and creed, and language, and uniting us in the bonds of eternal peace. I have looked even farther. I have speculated and probably dreamt, in the dim future—ay, a thousand years hence—I have speculated on what the effect of the triumph of this principle may be. I believe that the effect will be to change the face of the world, so as to introduce a system of government, entirely distinct from that which now prevails. I believe that the desire and the motive for large and mighty empires, for gigantic armies and

great navies—for those materials which are used for the destruction of life and the desolation of the rewards of labor will die away. I believe that such things will cease to be necessary, or to be used, when man becomes one family and freely exchanges the fruits of his labor with his brother man.

Free trade philosophy meant more than just trade, it meant a better organization of society and a better future for humankind, an ideal firmly held by Palmerston and most Victorians. The real debate lay in the question of intervention—where, when, and why to intervene. Palmerston interfered overseas to keep the balance of power, to promote free trade and keep open markets for British goods. This policy, Palmerston assured the public, meant that the best interest of Britain coincided with the best interests of the world. It was a very convenient belief, but one he sincerely held. The British kicked the door of trade open if foreign governments did not open their markets willingly, and Britain understood that it would reap the lion's share of economic opportunity because of its lead in the Industrial Revolution. The belief in free trade only deepened in the coming decades as Britain expanded around the world into services like banking and insurance, and forms of investments such as utility companies, ports, and railways. Though many Tories resisted the vision, drawn to the ideal of an insular England, the sentiment in favor of free trade became entrenched in British society and did not substantially wane until the depression of the 1930s.

Latin America

Many scholars claim Britain held an informal empire in Latin America. Palmerston did much to bring this about, but so too did other British officials who were interested in the region well before, and after, Palmerston's period in office. Competition between the United States, France, and Britain heightened the rush for influence in the region. In 1810, Britain signed a peace treaty with Brazil that gave preferential treatment to British interests. After this Britain intervened often in Latin America between the 1830s and 1860s to remove obstacles to trade, investment, and finance. When the Spanish colonies rebelled against Spain, Britain hesitated to recognize the new governments, due primarily to a sense of loyalty to the Spanish support of Britain against France during the Napoleonic wars. But when the British government finally recognized the independent republics, it did so by signing trade treaties. This amounted to holding out the carrot of recognition if the republics met Britain on the ground of open trade and thus opened their economies to British penetration. Britain also played an instrumental role in the creation of Uruguay as a buffer zone between Brazil and Argentina to guarantee open river systems for British trade in the region. Other intrusions to keep trade open occurred frequently up the River Platte and as far as Mexico. In 1848–49 Britain threatened naval action off the coast of Brazil to stop the trade in slaves and menaced Peru in

1857 to ensure her compliance for British bondholders, and then again against Chile in 1863, among other actions.

The battle for informal empire in Latin America did not mean that either the United States or Britain possessed an informal empire in Latin America before 1860 but rather that both nations engaged in informal imperialism in this era, the British more successfully than the Americans. Between 1812 and 1860, Britain's steady involvement formed the perimeters of the state, the economy, and eventually much of the elite of the region. Already in the eighteenth century, illicit trade by South Americans with Britain, in defiance of Spanish colonial monopolies, surpassed trade with the mother country. This whetted the appetite of British merchants and gave British officials an interest in formalizing and expanding a commercial exchange between the Spanish colonies and Britain. The Napoleonic wars provided the first opportunity to effect this change. When the crown of Spain allied with Napoleon, she towed her American colonies into the war with her and thus technically provided the British with an additional incentive and a legal excuse to strip away the Spanish colonies and integrate these regions deeper into the British economy—an economy exploding in manufacturing capabilities and in search of new outlets for a wide array of goods, with textiles in the lead.

A number of issues piqued British interest in the region. Illicit trade already existed between the former Spanish colonies and Britain. The region gave British officials every reason to hope for another success story mimicking that of North America as a neo-Europe, to use a modern phrase. The Platte region encompassed modern-day Argentina and Uruguay and attracted European settlers with its temperate conditions free from the tropical diseases that affected immigrants in India, Africa, and Brazil. Albeit the Spanish and Italians largely peopled the region, other Europeans lived there as well. The settlers practiced Catholicism—another drawback—but the combination of a temperate climate in a land peopled with Christian Europeans eager to trade with Britain and showing a remarkable interest in all things English made the region a tempting target for informal empire.

In the eighteenth century many in Britain believed the peoples of Latin America wanted to break free from the Spanish colonial yoke and trade openly with an industrializing England. The brief experience of Montevideo, in Uruguay, as an open port to the world made clear not only to the Montevideo citizens but also to British merchants that an opening of this region to free trade meant that the lion's share of trade would fall to England and open up a society ready to emulate British culture—a region to replace the lost formal empire of the United States with all the advantages of empire and none of the cost. Palmerston understood this well and knew that by excluding rivals from holding formal empire in the region Britain corralled the territory into her own sphere of influence.

Uruguay owes its existence to British ambition for informal empire. John Forbes, a U.S. envoy to Argentina, called it "a colony in disguise." When war broke out between Argentina and Brazil over the territory to the East of the Rio de la Plata, the Oriental Banda, the British saw the opportunities for extensive trade and influence wither away. In addition, the elites at Montevideo used the occasion for war to request that Britain admit their territory formally into the British empire. They wanted the stability, the trade, and the prestige that came with colonization. They wanted to be, in a word, British.

Canning's response in the 1820s lays the pattern that Palmerston and his successors at the Foreign Office followed well into the twentieth century and holds the key for understanding the utility of informal empire to the British in the nineteenth century. Canning declined the request to hold Uruguay as a former colony and chose instead to press for an agreement between Brazil and Argentina that created a buffer state open to British trade and immigration. The responsibility of formal empire avoided, Britain could enjoy the benefits of empire without the responsibility, including an outlet for manufactured products, loans, and immigrants. The finest port in the region lay available to the British as a naval stop as well as for trade, an outlet for the entire Platte river basin.

Other powers besides Britain and the United States showed intense interest in gaining influence in the region. For a decade throughout the 1830s France appeared to reap most of the benefits that Foreign Secretary Palmerston wanted for Britain. The influence of France flowed from the influx of French immigrants who outnumbered by far the British immigrants. The French government sent agents to establish closer diplomatic and military ties, particularly in Montevideo, and pressed for a special economic relationship that favored French products over the lower-priced British goods. Palmerston warned the French off, however, with the thinly veiled threat that "interference on the Part of French agents and commanders must tend to produce corresponding interference in the opposite Direction by the agents and forces of other Countries and thus to bring on a collision between France and other European powers."

While the British found the Platte region difficult to tame, they easily disposed of the French threat. A greater challenge to British hegemony arose with the "American System" promoted by the Americans in the North. This system found a southern parallel in the rise of Juan Manuel de Rosas, governor of Buenos Aires from 1820 to 1832 and 1835 to 1852, who, along with his supporters on the Pampas, no more desired a British informal empire in Argentina and Uruguay than earlier patriots desired Spanish supremacy. The same force of Creole rebellion to European hegemony resisted the British throughout the 1840s and kept Britain from realizing her ambition of making Latin America a mirror of England.

For the British the rise of Rosas occurred at the worst time. A cowboy revolution that saw Rosas and his supporters sweeping the liberal, pro–free market merchant elite out of Buenos Aries, and a powerful pro-Rosas faction in Montevideo supporting the same agenda—with defaulted loans, tariffs to keep out imported goods, and trade practically disappearing—made the British situation worse. The Industrial Revolution in Britain proceeded fitfully, with overproduction causing prices for textiles and other manufactured goods to fluctuate, high unemployment, massive social unrest due to rapid urbanization, and limited social services to care for the growing working class. Palmerston hoped, along with others, that expanding markets around the world, and certainly in the Platte region, would help to remedy the situation. While the foreign secretary and Governor Rosas often differed, Palmerston maintained a warm friendship with Rosas and they often exchanged letters. But Palmerston argued that if countries refused to join the family of responsible nations and trade accordingly, then a government like Britain should not only exercise the right but the responsibility to open up recalcitrant markets. James Murray in 1841 authored a Foreign Office study on the Platte region with the full agreement of Palmerston, and laid out a clear program for informal empire. Murray saw the Platte region "capable of consuming the greater part of what Great Britain even with its multiplying power of Steam can produce." It became incumbent upon Britain to take proactive steps to bring the region to heel. He wrote, laying out a clear formula for informal empire, that "Self-preservation, as it regards Great Britain, can scarcely be said to consist in only maintaining Political power, in the simple acceptance of the term, inasmuch as the Commercial interests of Great Britain are so mixed up with her Political strength, that it becomes necessary to support the one in order to maintain the other."

The interventions that followed show the ideas in action. The French initiated a blockade of Buenos Aires in March 1838, claiming the mistreatment of its nationals, of which ten thousand resided in Buenos Aires and two thousand in Montevideo. France opened hostilities with Rosas during the end of the province's brief period of ascendancy. French warships kept the Europhile elites on the coast and in the city from trading with Europe. Many of the merchants whose livelihood depended on trade moved to Montevideo and joined the efforts financed by the French to resist Rosas and keep Uruguay from falling under his sway. But the effort failed due to Rosas's strength in the countryside and because France lost interest and pulled support, warned off by Palmerston.

Lord Aberdeen, who would follow Palmerston as foreign secretary when Palmerston was temporarily out of the government, then acted to support the Europhile elites in Montevideo who held out against Rosas. He also acted to keep resistance in the city alive and open up the region once more for trade. Working jointly with the French, in September 1845 the British sailed into the harbor, erected a blockade on Buenos Aires, and then forced their way up the Parana River. Because Rosas denied foreign ships the right to navigate and trade on the Parana, the British in 1846 sailed upriver to a point called El Quebracho. Behind the war vessels sailed a convoy of merchant ships that landed at the city of Asuncion and promptly unloaded British manufactured goods for sale on the docks. No action could more directly illustrate the purpose of informal empire.

Eventually Rosas signed a treaty for the free navigation of the Parana and for the independence of Uruguay, with its open port of Montevideo, in 1849. While Britain took such care to keep its allies alive in Montevideo, the elites in

Uruguay, disappointed in their hopes of gaining the status of a British colony, pressed Britain to accept Uruguay as a protectorate. They sweetened the deal by offering Britain concessions for a more permanent involvement in the area. Palmerston resisted the allure, however, rejecting the overtures as "an embarrassing responsibility." When Palmerston returned to office in 1846, he decided to wrap up negotiations with Rosas and gain an agreement—without further intervention—to the dismay of Latin American allies.

The dream of a British informal empire in South America languished but did not die out. British influence still mattered, but in the 1850s and 1860s the paramount foreign power shifted temporarily to Brazil, which could provide money, mercenaries, agents, and ready diplomatic assistance to Uruguay. But the foundation of British influence had been lain, and with increased investment in infrastructure such as ports, railways, and, later, public utilities of every description, British influence grew throughout the century in Latin America, including Brazil, Chile, Peru, and Mexico. While scholars disagree on whether the term "informal empire" applies to British influence in Latin America, most agree that trade and influence grew noticeably throughout the Palmerstonian period and into the twentieth century, when the United States, with its great economic might, stepped in and replaced the British role in the region.

The Eastern Question

Many scholars have also asserted that Britain had an informal empire in the Middle East, particularly in Egypt and Turkey. The Eastern Question centered on the fate of the Ottoman empire, which ruled a significant portion of southeast Europe with 8 million European Christian subjects, most of them Slavic. Centered in Constantinople, now called Istanbul, the Ottoman empire also ruled most of North Africa, Egypt, the Middle East, and much of Persia, today called Iran. The Ottoman territory bumped up against Russia in the North and Austria in the northwestern part of the empire. This cauldron of peoples and cultures proved particularly hard for the traditional ruler of the Ottoman Turks, the Sultan, to manage. The instability of the region inspired hopes in a number of great powers that desired to carve up and absorb large chunks of the territory. Henry Bulwer, whom Palmerston appointed as Secretary of Embassy to Constantinople, summed up the British view of the situation before his arrival in terms with which Palmerston would have agreed heartily:

> Sultan Mahmoud still reigned over the terror of that city and its neighborhood; the plan he had deliberately and with no common determination of character formed—that of introducing amongst his subjects the civilization of Western Europe—was just beginning to execute itself. Prussian officers were drilling his troops, an English officer was instructing his Navy, and though the great bulk of the population wore their old magnificent costumes, their persons who held official employments were obliged to dismiss the turban for the fez (the red cap now in use) and to disfigure themselves in the frock coat they still wear.

From this paragraph alone one can see that the author saw the drive for Europeanization and the attempt to westernize the Turkish peoples as somewhat ridiculous, probably because of the emphasis on style over substance. Bulwer emphasized the importance of fiscal and administrative reforms over the wholesale abandonment of indigenous culture. But Palmerston, like most Europeans of the age, felt a certain disdain for the Turks, quipping that not much could be expected "from a nation who have no heels to their shoes and spend the whole of their life slipshod."

Russia particularly, but also Austria and France, hoped to carve the Turkish territory up and rule as imperial masters. Russia, whose access to the North Sea was prevented by ice in the winters, wanted to push south and take land that bordered on the Mediterranean, where it could trade and place warships to protect its interest. France dreamed of imperial glory in North Africa and Egypt. Austria wanted more influence and territory in the southeastern part of Europe. Constant insurrections among the Christian subjects of the region, particularly the Serbs, and a desire among the Christian nations to protect the interests of their fellow believers, furthered the ambitions of Austria in the Turkish territory. The weak government in Constantinople often severely mistreated the Serbs in a desperate bid to maintain control and keep the Austrians, and the Russians, who shared a common Slavic heritage with the Serbs, out of the region.

Against these European ambitions stood the British and Palmerston, who saw things differently. The Ottoman empire lay on the "route to India." Rival European powers that held any part of the Ottoman empire threatened British naval supremacy in the Mediterranean and had the ability to block supplies and soldiers by land. The British preferred the Turks, over whom they had great influence, holding the land route to the jewel in the crown, India.

Palmerston had every reason to worry about France. During the French Revolutionary War, France attempted to cut off British access to India by sending General Napoleon to Egypt with an army. Napoleon failed in his mission and withdrew in 1801. But during this time the elites of France and Egypt eyed each other with new interest. The French yearned to return to the region as a power. Fashion set the tone for ambition as all things Egyptian, from hookahs to pyramid motifs on furniture, became the rage, with many wealthier homeowners sporting a "Turkish corner" decorated with carpets, drapes, and brassware from the Ottoman empire, including Egypt. The infatuation went both ways, at least for Mehmit Ali (1769–1849). A former Albanian tobacco trader and a captain in the service of the Mamelukes, eunuch elites who ruled Egypt at the time of the French invasion, Ali watched in awe as superior artillery and gunfire obliterated the famous cavalry charges of the Mamelukes. When Ali came to power he launched a massive modernization program to reform the economy. With ambitions to expand the influence of Egypt and perhaps march on Istanbul and replace the Sultan himself, Ali modernized his economy to produce exports and to fund a new, stronger army.

Ali's economic program shocked many European observers. He abolished most private property, seized farmland from peasants and controlled the land directly by government agents, forcing the peasants to work as agricultural laborers with almost no real income in return. He also made them stop planting the varied agricultural products necessary for the local economy and instead to plant cotton, calling it the "New System." The exports brought in enough money for Ali to launch Western-style military reforms and massive building projects, for instance, building a new canal to connect the city of Alexandra to the Nile, a project that used the forced labor of twenty thousand workers. He even planned to tear down the pyramids and use the stones to line the canals, until horrified British and French officials talked him out of the scheme, thus saving the pyramids for future generations.

French officials advised Ali, French soldiers trained his army, and French merchandise flooded into Egypt. Palmerston worked to undo this French influence. But the British economy, without conscious planning by officials, changed the balance in favor of British power. Egypt under Mehmit Ali raised cotton to provide cash for the state. The textile mills that powered Britain's Industrial Revolution began purchasing the cotton produced by Egypt, and Britain moved ahead of France as Egypt's number one trading partner. Then, in 1838, Palmerston and his ambassador Henry Bulwer negotiated a treaty with the Ottoman empire that forced Ali to abandon his nationalized agriculture project.

This led to another unintended consequence that gave Britain even more influence in the region. Without income from nationalized agriculture, Ali began to take out government loans, raised in London and Paris, to continue his expensive efforts at modernization. In addition, Europeans negotiated the right of "capitulations," which included the right of foreigners to be tried in their own courts by European peers, thus making them feel safer, even immune from prosecution within the Ottoman empire. Foreigners flooded into Egypt to trade. In return for the loans that private investors made to Egypt, the government protected the capitalists by a free trade treaty with the Ottoman empire called the "Convention of Balta Liman," which gave control of customs and tariffs to a partnership of European countries. The income from customs then paid back the investors, with the remainder going to the government of Egypt and the Ottoman government in Constantinople. In this way, Britain and other European powers, particularly France, came to hold a great deal of influence in the Ottoman empire.

But in the 1840s Palmerston had managed to bar any substantial Russian and French influence in the Ottoman empire. One historian, Professor Driault, commented, "All the advantages had fallen to Britain. She had pushed back Mohammed Ali and France in the south, Russia in the North, and kept open for the future the overland route to India via Iraq. She had made safe the development of her influence along this route. She was preeminent in the lands of the Levant." One could add that Britain triumphed in another way too. Free trade treaties had given Britain economic dominance in the Ottoman empire as well. Palmerston played a major role in constructing this empire of trade and influence.

The first major military engagement in the region required Palmerston to make a choice between Mehmit Ali, the Pasha of Egypt, and the Sultan in Constantinople, or "the Porte," as diplomats referred to the capital of the Ottoman empire. The Sultan had called on his Pasha for help in his conflict with the independence movement in Greece, and Ali had agreed to provide both an army and a fleet. The British felt much sympathy with the liberty-loving Greeks, and sent in the navy to sink the Egyptian fleet in the battle at Navarino. The Sultan lost control over the Morea—that part of Greece that attained some degree of independence. This disappointed Ali because his deal with the Sultan included the Morea as payment for his fleet and army. Instead he entered Syria for payment and sent a representative in 1831 to the Sultan to gain his approval for his actions. The Sultan exploded in rage at this insolent move and sent instead of approval an invasion force to defeat Ali. Ali's army decimated the Sultan's forces, once, and then twice. The road from Syria to the Porte lay wide open. Palmerston at this juncture had to choose sides in this internal squabble within the Ottoman empire.

The foreign secretary felt that this instability endangered the "avenues to India." The sea route to India round the southern horn of Africa forced sailing vessels to make a long and arduous detour. But only two shorter land routes remained feasible. One involved disembarking passengers and goods at the narrow land bridge of Suez and moving them overland to the Red Sea, sailing from there to India; or to a more northern route, through Asia Minor and down the Euphrates River to the Persian Gulf. The northern route meant moving through the Sultan's territory, and also placing the route perilously close to Russia, which, the British feared, sought dominance in the area. But the southern route through Suez meant going through the territory of Ali. Ali, however, unlike the Sultan, resisted British overtures while his realm crawled with Frenchmen and the influence they brought to bear.

Palmerston sought to throw his weight behind the Sultan and drive Ali back into Egypt. But Lord Grey, the prime minister, and the rest of the cabinet demurred. Britain had already overextended its navy: on the North Sea, watching over the Dutch; on the Continent supervising a diplomatic sparring match between Belgium and Spain; and in India, where Russia, so the British thought, extended influence on the Northwestern Frontier in Afghanistan, hoping for the chance to grab a client state in the region and have an informal empire that one day touched the warm waters of the Indian Ocean. Handcuffed, Palmerston fumed at the inaction that he felt endangered the peace of Europe and the balance of power. It created a vacuum of power in the region. Russia, as Palmerston feared, then moved in gladly to protect the Sultan from invasion. When the Russians finally left the Ottoman empire, they only did so with a treaty called the Treaty of Unkiar Skelessi, which haunted Palmerston for eight years. The treaty contained a clause that required the Sultan to consult Russia on all internal affairs.

Palmerston worried about the clause and the Russians. Slowly, he turned against Russian influence in this quarter. Some attribute this to his falling out with Princess Lieven. But Russian brutality in Poland probably had more to do with it and did much to turn the press in England anti-Russian and thus brought Palmerston, ever sensitive to the newspapers, along with the tide. He argued in cabinet that things had gone from bad to worse after Ali's invasion of Syria. The Russians had gained more influence in the Porte, and any alliance of influence between France and Russia could wrest all power in the Levant out of British hands completely. He responded by asserting the "integrity" of the Ottoman empire. Britain must, he argued, hold the ramshackle Ottoman empire together so that it had the power to exclude outside influence. Only this would keep the route to India safe. With the backing of Lord Grey, he then worked to get Ali out of Syria, forcing him back into his "original shell of Egypt." He instructed his ambassador in Constantinople, Lord Ponsonby, to assure the Porte of British support against Ali, adding, "We shall probably send our squadron to Alexandria and Syria, in company with some part of the French ships of war, to give Mehemet an outward and visible sign of our inward intentions on this subject."

It took eight years to accomplish this. Working tirelessly with other European powers, Palmerston succeeded in getting Ali to agree to halt his expansions, and in return the Sultan recognized his rule in Syria and adjoining areas, including Mecca. But two problems haunted Ali and made his occupation of Syria impossible. Ali strained to supply his army, as Palmerston foresaw, which maneuvered far from home, and his autocratic methods of government monopolies angered Syrians, Druze, and Arabs, who at first welcomed him as a deliverer from the rule of the Turks, and then felt the lash of his harsh methods. Finally, in 1839, Palmerston succeeded in patching together a "European concert" (excluding France) to agree with Ali to make his family the hereditary rulers of Egypt but requiring them to withdraw back into Egypt.

The Pacifico Affair

The Eastern Question served as a backdrop to one of the most dramatic foreign policy showdowns in Palmerston's life; the Don Pacifico affair. This public scuffle showed Palmerston at his best and at his worst and illustrated a "Palmerstonian" moment, which drew the attention of the nation and the world. In this incident he tackled a point of justice that had little support at home and abroad, used the Royal Navy to force the capitulations of a foreign government over a point of disagreement, and then faced a frenzy of opposition for his actions. Many journalists and parliamentarians assumed the affair would finish Palmerston's career. But in a single night he persuaded the public and the Parliament by brilliant—and prolonged—oratory, to support him. It ended as a high-water mark that carried him, a few years later, to the office of prime minister. Unfortunately even admirers of Palmerston admit that in this affair he unleashed a drama of titanic proportions onto the world stage merely to protect what must certainly have been a charlatan, a man named David Pacifico, who went by the title of "Don" Pacifico.

Pacifico had served the government of Portugal as a consul official in Morocco (1835–37) and then for a brief time as consul in Greece. After his dismissal from office he stayed in Greece and lived as a merchant. A few years before the incident Lionel de Rothschild had visited Greece. Rothschild had arranged special loans for the Greek government. Partially to honor their Jewish visitor, the Greek government banned the annual burning of an effigy of Judas Iscariot that occurred between Easter Sunday and Pentecost. When the festival passed without the normal ritual an enraged mob attacked the house of Don Pacifico, a Jew, in revenge.

Pacifico sought compensation from the Greek government for his losses, which the government refused. Because he had been born in 1784 in Gibraltar, he technically was a British citizen and so he applied to the British government to help him urge his case for compensation. After Thomas Wyse, the British official responsible for issues of compensation, turned down his request for help, Pacifico shrewdly sent a letter to Palmerston. This tactic may not have worked with most foreign secretaries, but as Palmerston read a voluminous amount of incoming letters and dispatches he read the letter personally, deciding to make the cause of Pacifico the cause of international justice and British liberty. The only problem: European treaties delegated the management of affairs in Greece to Britain, France, and Russia. Thus Palmerston did not have the legal or moral authority to act alone. Additionally Pacifico claimed enormous sums, most of it spurious.

A little context explains Palmerston's actions. Other conflicts with the Greek government had arisen—small ones—that irritated Palmerston's sense of justice. The Greek government had earned a reputation for brutality and extreme corruption. Recently, when the crew of a British naval vessel, the *Fantome,* had entered the Greek port of Patras to resupply, local police had arrested the crew, roughed them up, and thrown them into jail for a night. Other British citizens in Greece had been robbed and unable to get redress from the government, or in one case, property lines moved indiscriminately without compensation, cutting off a homeowner's garden and leaving only the house. Palmerston knew of these outrages and no doubt had already felt annoyed by the time he received the letter from Pacifico.

Further, the issue involved a larger principle, never clearly articulated in British history. Palmerston believed the citizens of the British empire had the same rights and privileges as the citizens of ancient Rome who expected the law to protect them wherever they traveled. This assertion by Palmerston had high romantic appeal to the British people, particularly the educated elite who read as schoolboys Cicero's famous remark that the phrase "Civis Romanus sum" [I am a Roman citizen] always protected Romans from outrage even "in the remotest parts of the earth." The British also understood the biblical undertones to the issue from the book of Acts in the New Testament. When the Apostle Paul, arrested and beaten, declared he held the status of freeborn Roman citizen, his captors trembled at their own misbehavior—Roman law prescribed the death penalty for maltreating a citizen. Palmerston, asserting the same principle, appealed to the patriotism of his listeners—was not the British empire, he thundered, as great as the Roman empire?

Springing into action, Palmerston ordered Admiral Parker, commanding the Mediterranean fleet of British battleships guarding the Dardanelles, to sail for Athens and blockade all shipping to and from Greece. This Palmerston did without consulting the two other European powers that by treaty oversaw the autonomy of Greece from the Ottoman empire—France and Russia. They of course protested, and the British Parliament considered a motion to censure Palmerston. Always seen as pushing things too fast, too recklessly in foreign affairs, it appeared that this time he had gone too far and that he deserved his comeuppance and a public censure.

But that did not happen. In Parliament Palmerston spoke from ten in the evening till two the next morning. By the time he sat down, as Lord Clarendon's wife, Katherine explained to a friend, Palmerston had "triumphed over a great mass of educated public opinion, over that mighty potentate the Times, and over two branches of the Legislature, over the Queen and Prince, and most of the Cabinet he sits in, besides all foreign nations." In one speech, quietly delivered, he had swung the country entirely behind him in a flood of applause.

In his speech he gave a sweeping defense of his foreign policy and some background to the difficulties in Greece. He reminded his colleagues that in 1828—eight years after Greece had revolted from Turkey—England, France, and Russia had ultimately decided to force Turkey to acknowledge Greece's independence, and that in 1832 a treaty was signed to that effect, acknowledging a parliamentary form of government and a constitutional monarchy. Unfortunately, the constitutional forms of government did not protect the people of Greece or foreigners who necessarily reside there from the kind of brutal and corrupt behavior that the former Turkish overlords had once practiced. "In all times, in Greece, as is well known, there has prevailed, from the daring habits of the people, a system of compulsory appropriation—forcible appropriation by one man of that which belonged to another" and this had hurt the social condition of the country, hurt the prospects for improvement, and hurt prosperity. He declared that what "foreigners call brigandage" has now grown worse, not better, under Greek leadership.

He then concluded his speech with an almost irresistible appeal to patriotism and justice, invoking the grandeur of the Roman empire and the liberties of citizenship that Roman citizens enjoyed. The comparison flattered his listeners and the British public, by reminding them that Britain had attained similar heights of power, prestige, and influence. To disagree with Palmerston would have meant denying the greatness of imperial Britain, a point he drove home brilliantly by again using the Latin phrase, familiar to all his listeners in parliament, "I am a Roman Citizen."

> I therefore fearlessly challenge the verdict which this House, as representing a political, a commercial, a constitutional country, is to give on the question now brought before it; whether the principles on which the foreign policy of Her Majesty's Government has been conducted, and the sense of duty which has led

us to think ourselves bound to afford protection to our fellow subjects abroad, are proper and fitting guides for those who are charged with the Government of England; and whether, as the Roman, in days of old, held himself free from indignity, when he could say Civis Romanus sum; so also a British subject, in whatever land he may be, shall feel confident that the watchful eye and the strong arm of England, will protect him against injustice and wrong.

Palmerston turned a potential disaster into a political triumph. While his actions also increased resentment around the world for Britain's high-handed hijacking of legal and moral principles, these same actions also increased the prestige and power of Britain. Power equals prestige—one of the reasons why Palmerston so rarely turned down an opportunity to display British might. In many ways, the informal empire of trade that he did so much to promote, as well as the swollen and growing British empire, depended upon the slender, silver strand of prestige that tied it all together. He feared that without the prestige and the force that backed it up, Britain's influence in the world would quickly fade.

Africa

Palmerston did not display British power only for prestige and trade, however. He passionately opposed the slave trade and led the fight between 1840 and 1860 for the British campaign against human bondage in Africa. Parliament made the slave trade in the British colonies and the transport of slaves in British ships illegal in 1807. The practice of slavery itself came to an official end in 1833. But antislavery circles in Britain wanted to snuff out the slave trade that still continued in Africa. Africans, Arabs, and Portuguese trafficked in black slaves, most of them bound for the plantations in Brazil.

Africans had long engaged in slavery in the domestic market, but selling slaves abroad meant income to buy European clothes, which Africans wore as novelty items and as status symbols. They also bought alcohol and, most importantly, guns. Tribal leaders who succeeded in plugging into the new globalization that began with the massive commercial European empires could outcompete those leaders who did not. Slaves became an important way to gain guns and, through guns, power and empire.

The quest for guns and other Western commodities stimulated not only slave trading but also the import of European farming, from cattle and sheep grazing to corn, rice, and nuts. Locals purchased these goods and also traded in the port cities and with the growing economic powerhouse in the south, the Cape colony. Europeans readily paid for African commodities like ivory, honey, and furs. European demand for billiard balls and piano keys made of ivory provided a ready market for elephant tusks. Palm oil was one of the most important commodities, whose trade increased from a few thousand tons a year in the 1820s to in excess of 30,000 tons by the early 1850s. Precious metals, diamonds, leather hides, and wild rubber all spurred white expansion inland, particularly from the Cape. Missionaries like David Livingston promoted these economic changes along with the propagation of Christianity. And Africans migrated toward the south and the growing coastal cities looking for jobs and economic opportunity.

The British government grew increasingly powerful in Africa as the nineteenth century progressed. Britain held a dominant role in the coastal regions of West Africa early in the eighteenth century, and this included a mix of formal and informal empire, the latter covering more territory and eliciting more trade than the former. The British maintained trading stations between Senegambia (in the west) and the Niger delta (in the east), with a presence in the Gold Coast that went back one hundred years.

While Britain sought trade and influence, it also sought to end the slave trade for moral reasons. Palmerston signed a series of treaties with African rulers to suppress the slave trade and, significantly, to open up and safeguard legitimate trade. The extension of formal colonies had become a redundancy for the British in Africa. Britain preferred informal influence to formal control. Formal colonies did not cover most of the continent until competition with other European powers led in the 1880s to the "Scramble for Africa," in which almost the whole of Sub-Saharan Africa was carved up into formal colonies. In Africa, unlike Latin America, informal control preceded formal control.

The Palmerston era saw British influence radiating out from the city of Lagos in Nigeria, with navy cruisers patrolling the vast coast of western Africa. After Palmerston entered the Foreign Office in 1830, the British brokered treaties on the coasts, largely for the purpose of putting down the slave trade. Palmerston urged the Royal Navy not only to seize slave ships but also to make attacks on shore as a preventative policy. An attack on Bonny in 1836, in the Gallinas River in 1840, and blockades of Dahomey after 1850 typify this aggressive policy. Palmerston saw slaving as a "foul and detestable crime," the suppression of which conferred not only a moral blessing but also guaranteed that "the greatest commercial benefit would accrue, not to England only, but to every civilized nation." He believed this because where slavery stopped Africans then engaged in other diverse economic activities that profited all concerned.

When African rulers signed treaties with the British government they committed to a broad range of policies that went far beyond the issue of selling slaves. These treaties involved free trade principles enforced by the Royal Navy. Rulers often received stipends, putting the ruling elite of much of the West African coast, not yet under formal colonial rule, on the payroll of Britain. Another use for the navy, besides suppressing slavery and ensuring the safety of ships engaged in legitimate trade, included backing up consuls who engaged in the collection of debt. The Foreign Office appointed consuls to ensure the chiefs followed through with the terms of the treaties. These are a few convincing examples of informal empire.

Private expeditions, patronized by the government, pushed into Niger in 1841 and 1857, Dahomey in 1850, and Lagos in 1851 (which the British annexed in 1861). None of this activity meant Britain wanted formal colonies in the region.

Palmerston turned down opportunities for new formal colonies—in Abyssinia in the 1840s as well as for an earlier occupation in Egypt in 1859. What Palmerston said of Abyssinia, now called Ethiopia, expressed his sentiments toward most of Africa: "All we want is trade and land is not necessary for trade; we can carry on commerce very well on ground belonging to other people."

Much of the work of suppressing the slave trade in West Africa involved stopping the Portuguese from transporting slaves to Brazil. But East Africa offered a different set of challenges. By the time the British competed for influence in East Africa, the area had already fallen under the sway of the Arab sultan of Muscat (today Oman), who made the headquarters of his African empire in Zanzibar, the small island off the coast of Tanganyika (today Tanzania). Oman had an extensive fleet for shipping as well as for war and oversaw a substantial trade that linked India, Arabia, and Africa. Oman had large date plantations and imported about five hundred slaves a year from Africa. By 1744, Oman controlled not only Zanzibar but also the port cities of Mombassa, Lamu, Pemba, and Kilwa. Slaves became an export, with three thousand shipped per year, as well as sugar and cloves. To keep the slave supply going, traders delved deep into Africa, setting up camps around Lake Nyssa and Malawi.

In 1792, the Sultan in Oman signed a Treaty of Commerce and Navigation with Britain. The treaty authorized the British to shut down the slave trade in east Africa, certainly one of the main reasons for the agreement. But military strategy played a key role in the treaty as well, and the idea of informal empire in the region percolated in the minds of adventurers, businessmen, missionaries, and government officials alike. Napoleon had entertained plans for marching through Oman on his way to India, and the British wanted to offer protection to Oman in return for a pledge to ally with Britain in any conflict involving India. Britain had another concern as well. The growing wealth of the trading ports on Africa's east coast promised increased trade, and a market for goods emanating from British India. Ruling through the Sultan of Oman therefore made sense. Suppression of slavery provided the key that unlocked the door of influence in East Africa. Yet paradoxically, the impulse for suppression did not arise merely from the motive for power or business. Many of the allies the British had in Africa and the Middle East resented the crusade against slavery. The insistence on stamping out slavery in East Africa sometimes cut against trade, and it arose from a moral vision that overrode all objections.

China

Africa and the Middle East did not present the same set of problems that Palmerston encountered in many other parts of the globe. He could not, for instance, micromanage affairs in the Far East because distance delayed communication. The Foreign Office tolerated far more independence from officials and expected them to act on their own, which led, inevitably, to more "gunboat diplomacy" and intervention. This proved especially the case with China, where the East India Company carried on a lucrative trade exchanging, for the most part, opium grown and processed in India, for tea. In 1834 Britain lifted the East India Company's monopoly on trade. Many in the West and in China used opium as a medicine, but many also became addicted to the drug, and Chinese society suffered from widespread use. But when the Chinese government attempted to ban the import of opium, British officials balked at the suggestion. First the Chinese did not also attempt to ban domestic production of poppies and the manufacture of opium, giving the impression to the British that Chinese officials angled for an unfair trade advantage. In addition the British sold their opium in chests to smugglers who brought the drug into the mainland or through smugglers and corrupt Chinese officials in Canton, the only official trading station in which the Imperial Chinese government allowed the British and other foreigners to set up shop as merchants. They also required foreign merchants to sell their goods exclusively through the "Co-hong," a select guild of Chinese merchants. If the British had ceased to import opium, not only would China have continued with its domestic market, but smugglers along the Chinese coast would simply have purchased the drug elsewhere, leaving the lucrative trade in the hands of competitors.

Even these reasons did not fully explain Palmerston's refusal to ban the importation of opium. The British imported tea, an expensive item, in large quantities from China. And until the opium trade arose in sufficient quantities, the British paid for tea with hard currency, silver, on the demand of the Chinese government. But since China purchased very few items in return from the West, currency then entered China and never circulated back out; this would have devastating consequences to the British, as well as the European and American economies—in fact most of the trading partners in the world. A shortage of currency translates in modern terms into high interest rates—a short money supply meant loans at high cost and a slowdown in economic activity. To ban opium would have resulted in one of two things—a severe slowdown in the economic growth of Britain and much of the world, or the need to abolish all trade with China to restore the balance.

Palmerston of course had no intention of letting that happen. He wanted China to "grow up" and join other nations in responsible diplomatic and trade relationships. He thought, as did many Europeans at the time, that nonwhites were childlike and required the cultural training of Western standards and norms over a long period of time to be properly developed. This understanding grew easily out of cultural chauvinism and commonly held racial stereotypes.

China, however, had an entirely different perspective. For a thousand years China had ruled as the superpower of Asia, exporting Buddhism, silk, writing, merchants, ceramics, and high culture. The Chinese saw outsiders as racially inferior barbarians, and tolerated them only to the extent that they paid tribute and respect to the emperor. When the Europeans began trading on the coasts of China, the government limited their intercourse—for the most part—to the city of Canton and refused to accept ambassadors to the court in Peking, keeping the west at a distance. China had no official diplomatic relations with any country of the world.

Chinese officials kept merchants at a distinct disadvantage, and British businessmen complained often to Palmerston of their humiliating treatment in Canton. A crisis arose, however, when the government of China attempted to collect tribute from the foreign merchants and also to seize a very lucrative cargo of opium. The British superintendent stationed in Canton, Captain Elliot of the Royal Navy, felt that the outrages had reached a limit and called a squadron of British naval vessels into the port. The British government demanded redress for the seized cargo and better treatment for Western prisoners. When the Chinese government insisted on seizing and trying British sailors for a charge of murder and surrounded the British squadron with twenty-nine naval vessels (junks), Captain Elliot instantly sank the Chinese fleet and captured key ports on the coast. The British gained from the Chinese government five treaty ports where they and other foreigners could trade. Many scholars argue that Shanghai became part of the British informal empire at this time. They also gained, formally, the island of Hong Kong, which became integrated into the formal British empire.

This conflict, called the Opium War of 1839–42, gained for the British the Treaty of Nanking (1842), which formalized the new privileges gained. Palmerston defended the British action to his critic Gladstone by saying that no man could "with a grave face" say that the Chinese government cared about the "promotion of moral habits" but rather, by not forbidding the growth of poppies within China, showed that "this was an exportation of bullion question, an agricultural interest-protection question . . . the poppy interest in China." The British did not fight only for their own interest, he argued, but to insist that the rights they won by treaty applied to all trading partners.

Palmerston had more reasons to fight China than a point of honor. China had 350 million inhabitants that he wanted to bring into the empire of trade. One biographer, Jasper Ridley, quotes Palmerston in a letter to Lord Auckland in 1841, explaining Britain's stake in the conflict.

> The Rivalship of European manufactures is fast excluding our productions from the markets of Europe, and we must unremittingly endeavor to find in other parts of the world new vents for the produce of our industry. The world is large enough and the wants of the human race ample enough to afford a demand for all we can manufacture; but it is the business of the Government to open and to secure the roads for the market. Will the navigation of the Indus turn out to be as great a help as was expected for our commerce? If it does, and if we succeed in our China expedition, Abyssinia, Arabia, the countries on the Indus and the new markets of China, will at no distant period give a most important extension to the range of our foreign commerce.

Trade depended upon trading partners, and Palmerston had no intention of letting "small wars" stand in the way.

4

Painting the Map Red

When Prince Albert, the royal consort of Victoria, died in 1861, Queen Victoria decided to build a fitting memorial to the man she loved and whose counsel had so often guided her. Albert supported the traditional monarchs of Europe and pushed for a more conservative foreign policy than Palmerston liked. But historians also credit Albert for toning down the aggressive edge that Palmerston brought to international affairs and, most notably, for his intervention with London and Washington that helped avoid war between Britain and the United States during the American Civil War. The Albert Memorial, completed in 1876 by the architect Gilbert Scott, illustrated Britain's role in the world. Albert sat facing south, appropriately the direction where so much of the global empire lay. The sculptor Henry Armstead depicted the royal consort larger than life seated under a canopy topped by a towering spire and cross. He majestically surveyed the world at his feet, holding in his hand the catalog of the Great Exhibition of 1851 that both he and the queen loved to visit and where, in the Crystal Palace, multiple exhibits dramatically portrayed the progress of British science, culture, and government. Around the base of the canopy are figures representing four continents: a buffalo for America, a camel for Africa, an elephant for Asia, and a bull for Europe. Also represented are groupings of figures for agriculture, engineering, and the manufacturing arts, all of which symbolize the peoples and cultures of an empire grateful to Albert and by implication the British people.

Palmerston would never have questioned these sentiments. Such values as those expressed in the Albert Memorial also help explain the support that the public gave a foreign policy that slowly had been "painting the map red" for the last 350 years—an expansion quickly reaching a crescendo in the latter part of the nineteenth century. Today empire is often condemned as the application of violence for the domination of others for greed and power. Though some Victorians certainly agreed with this, particularly the radicals in Parliament, most British citizens from the elite to the working class saw empire in quite different terms. Empire was the extension of power based on the sacrifice of patriotic citizens for the betterment of less fortunate areas of the world. The

Victorian conception of empire had more to do with modern doctrines of "development" than with brutality. British power rested on the prestige that came with these ideas and the fact that many of the peoples of the world agreed. Otherwise the domination of such large areas such as India and West Africa by this small island nation would have been wholly inconceivable.

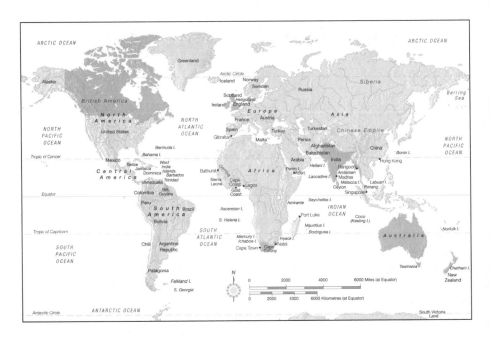

The Formal British Empire

The British empire grew substantially over the course of Palmerston's life and evolved differently in various regions of the globe. Historians often divide the formal empire into the first and second empires—the first, before the loss of the American colonies that became the United States, considered a mercantilist empire, while the second, which grew substantially in the nineteenth century, considered an empire of free trade. While this is not strictly true of either— mercantilism and free trade certainly overlapped at the time of the American Revolution—it does generally describe two approaches to empire. Historians sometimes discuss a third British empire, which followed World War I and emphasized trusteeship that prepared the regions ruled for eventual self-government.

Palmerston grew up in the eighteenth century, when Britain had a mercantile empire. A mercantile empire is one of masterful commercial control that generally does not allow the colony to trade outside the mother country. This benefits the mother country because it guarantees a supply of raw material, and it benefits the colony because it means a guaranteed market. Britain had exactly such an empire in India and other parts of the world, and this was not abolished, in India for instance, until 1833.

While a number of policy changes characterize the second empire, none illustrates this better than the crusade against slavery that became a prominent feature of the Victorian empire. Slavery made economic sense for the mercantilist empire and far less sense for the empire of free trade. The British colonial islands in the Caribbean provide a good example. The sugar plantations there depended on the importation of slaves who were forced into hard work with very little pay. The plantation owners made great profits importing sugar into Britain and from there into Europe. The price of labor skyrocketed when, through the efforts of men like Samuel Wilberforce, Parliament abolished the slave trade in 1807, and then abolished slavery altogether in 1833. To the frustration of the plantation owners Britain also allowed the importation of sugar from slave-run plantations in Brazil and thus undercut the market for Caribbean sugar even more. Once the richest and most valued part of the first empire, the Caribbean islands became the slums of the second empire.

The roll call of territories that Britain held by the time Palmerston became prime minister in 1855 covers a substantial portion of the land surface of the world. In the sixteenth century England expanded into the Caribbean with Barbados and the Bermudas. In the North, Britain expanded into New England and Nova Scotia and the Northwest Territories—what came to be called Canada. In West Africa, the British presence moved into Gambia and the Gold Coast. In the eighteenth century Britain expanded in North America to include New Brunswick, Prince Edward Island, Ontario, and Quebec, as well as the thirteen colonies that became the United States. It gained Gibraltar, the southern tip of Spain, and more islands in the Caribbean, such as Dominica, St. Vincent, Grenada, and Tobago. More territory in West Africa was added in the nineteenth century, in addition to gains in Australia, New Zealand, and Ceylon, with added territorial expansion over the whole of what is today India, Pakistan, and Bangladesh.

The empire had three main distinctions, one that in the latter half of the nineteenth century came to be called the Dominions, and one called the colonial empire, with India in its own category. This distinction paints with a wide brush, since the British empire was a patchwork of special arrangements, differing from region to region. The colonial empire was ruled directly by the colonial office, with a "steel frame," as the scholar Roger Louis says, of governors, administrators, courts, and military and police officials who oversaw all the operations of the government and the trade issues that tied it to Britain and the world. But while there were always similarities in structure, each region had different arrangements. In British India, for instance, much of the territory was ruled directly, but much of India was also ruled indirectly through the native princes who worked with, and under, the authority of the Indian government.

The Dominions were largely settled by whites from the British Isles and given a far greater degree of autonomy. The British government saw them as "New Britains" filled with enterprising Anglo-Saxons who took the prototype of

British race and culture into a new setting, creating variations on an English theme. Contemporaries of Palmerston believed that Anglo-Saxons took on a variety of minor characteristics in a new part of the world while remaining true to the essential racial type. For instance, many thought Canada bred Anglo-Saxons as an active, hardy breed of somewhat smaller stature; Australia bred Anglo-Saxons as intellectually active, a somewhat nervous type, tall, thin, and pale, rather like a stalk of corn. South Africa produced a lithe, hard body tanned by the sun, while New Zealand tended to reproduce exactly the conditions of Britain and thus the exact characteristics in the Anglo-Saxons of England. The theme throughout this typology is that Anglo-Saxons in the Dominions were grown up, not children needing oversight, and thus deserving of self-government.

Canada first gained self-government and served as the role model for the other Dominions. When rebellions in 1837 threatened to see Canada leave the British empire as the thirteen American colonies had done previously, Lord Durham, a prominent Whig politician, came to Canada as governor-general. Durham strongly believed that decentralization of power did not weaken but preserved the empire. He issued the "Durham Report" in 1839 that advocated self-government, a proposal not actually implemented until 1846. Between this date and 1860, many colonial states in what is today Australia and South Africa also gained self-government. The British government expected the Dominions to be the pillars of its empire and a free association based on race and trade.

India and the rest of the colonies were in a different category altogether, India with its own structure, and the crown colonies with another. Britain expanded its power over the subcontinent through outright conquest, but not in a single expansion—from trading posts in Bombay and Calcutta it slowly acquired supremacy over the Indian peninsula against the fading power of the Mughal emperor, the Hindu states, and other colonial powers. After the crown took over from the East India Company in 1858, Britain ruled with a tighter hand, building roads, railways, military bases, and architectural structures that reinforced British supremacy and made the colony safer from rebellion.

The Secretary of State for India was a member of the British cabinet. His office and staff were located at the India Office in London. He presented to Parliament annually the budget of the Indian government and gave a report on its conditions and progress. Any law passed by the Indian government went through the Secretary of State for India and through the council that he oversaw. Under him ruled the viceroy, who lived in India. The viceroy ruled with the power of a monarch even though his policy decisions still had to clear a council in India and the Secretary of State for India, who himself based his decisions on the cabinet and the advice of the prime minister and Parliament. The distance between India and Britain and the difficulties of communication gave the viceroy a theater of operation that compared favorably to that of a supreme ruler. The use of term "viceroy" for the governor-general of India was meant to convey the idea that the governor-general represented the monarch. Before the

British government took over direct rule of India from the East India Company, the term "governor-general" had referred to the head of the East India Company

The crown colonies, that is, those territories that were not the Dominions and not India, were governed from 1801 to 1854 by the Secretary of State for War (not Palmerston's old position, which was Secretary at War), and this cabinet position also served as the Secretary of State for the Colonies. During the Crimean War the position of Secretary at War was eliminated, with its responsibilities taken over by the Secretary of State for War, and a new position came into being to govern the crown colonies—the Secretary of State for the Colonies. His office and staff were located near the Prime Minister's Office on Downing Street. This new position was a member of the cabinet and held great power, including the ability to overrule any law passed by a colonial legislator. The territories that the position oversaw were immense and stretched from Africa, the Mediterranean, and the Far East to Latin America. While the Secretary of State for War had also formally overseen the Dominions as well, he exercised in practice far less authority in these regions than in the crown colonies.

Between the Dominions, India, and the crown colonies, a quarter of the land surface of the earth was included in the British empire. The chain of command for this empire was complex: the governors of the white Dominions were appointed by the crown at the advice of the prime minister and answered to the colonial secretary, who answered to the prime minister and the cabinet; India was governed by the viceroy and his council, and answered to the Secretary of State for India, who in turn answered to the prime minister and the cabinet; the crown colonies were governed by a wide range of officials, usually called governors, who also answered to the Secretary of State for the Colonies. And running as supporting beams through this whole structure was the Foreign Office, run by the foreign secretary, and the navy, and the army. All answered to the prime minister, who then answered to Parliament. Settlers, business interests, and the activities of the church added support to this whole structure and were in fact the reason for the existence of the empire.

Those who dissented from the prevailing positive view of the British empire voiced their opposition not just in Britain but also often in remote parts of the British empire itself. When the colonies of North America rebelled, that was a form of resistance, as was the Indian Mutiny of 1857. But resistance took many forms, as did collaboration with the British. In India for instance, the response to British power was complex. There were in the 1830s only forty-five thousand British in the Indian empire ruling over 150 million Indians. This would have been impossible without Indian collaboration. Collaboration and resistance changed not only how the British managed the empire but also changed the traditional societies that the British ruled.

Two trends can be identified in the Indian empire that changed both how the British administered the empire and how the Indians changed in response: westernization and orientalism. In the first, officials of the East India Company tried to reform Indian society and make it reflect the values of the British. The cult of Thuggee was suppressed, a caste that murdered travelers on the roads of India. Suttee, the tradition that allowed and sometimes encouraged widows to burn themselves alive on the funeral pyre of their husbands, was outlawed. Thomas Macaulay, a historian and a Member of Parliament who also went to India as a member of the Governor-General's Council in 1834, advocated teaching English to Indians and helped introduce a Western system of law that is still in use today. He worked with a class of Indian collaborators who would be "English in taste, in opinions, in morals and in intellect." But the legal reforms went much further than banning certain cultural practices. The British introduced the concept of "absolute property" that forever changed the feudal relationships between peasants and traditional rulers. The goal of the British rulers in India was not just to secure the Pax Britannica in the subcontinent and an empire of trade but the Civis Britannica too, a cultural empire.

Some scholars claim that orientalism played a role in British rule as well. In this argument, the Anglicization of India went hand in hand with promoting a static, traditional view of India as "other" that emphasized the immutability of the caste system and the distance between Brahmins and the Sudras in a village system seen as ancient, agrarian, unchanging, and eternal. This "Orientalists" believed must be preserved if authentic Indian culture was to survive. Both views, westernization that sought to reform India and orientalism that sought to preserve aspects of Indian culture, influenced British administration of India.

The British empire should not be thought of as a monolithic structure, a single entity, with little internal differences. Often empire is thought of as a uniquely male construct, with white males conquering a darker-skinned people who are the "natives," who then become servants, in a land full of jungles, tigers, and exotic adventures. To a point this simplistic picture is true, but British women also engaged in the building of empire, traveling overseas as wives and mothers who inculcated in colonial families the values of patriotism, Christian faith, and racial superiority over nonwhite peoples. Women also served as missionaries, teachers, and nurses in India, Africa, and the Far East. The empire attracted academics bent on research, such as botanists and adventurers escaping boredom, and sexual minorities hoping for more freedom abroad than could be found in Victorian England. Many different Europeans were attracted to the British empire for a variety of reasons, though clearly trade played the central and organizing role in the interchange between the West and the non-West.

But the empire itself was riven with divisions and should not be thought of as a monolithic block. The northern parts of India were populated by lighter-skinned people who tended to dominate the darker-skinned Dravidian peoples of the south. The Dravidians had been overrun by Aryan invasions that occurred in multiple waves thousands of years before and whose descendents adopted the caste system to keep racially pure. Other invasions from Afghanistan and Persia left an enduring mark, including the old Mughal empire's destruction of much of Hindu culture in the north, tearing down the ancient temples in Banares and establishing themselves as brutal overlords. The Mughal empire also initiated the enlightened and tolerant reign of Akbar, who fostered toleration between different faiths. When the British came they found collaborators among many groups who preferred British overlords to the corrupt Mughal overlords in Delhi. India in the Victorian period was riven by caste divisions with distinct gender roles. Women had few rights, and racism was practiced at almost every level of society. India was and still is a diverse community with a mix of ancient cultures and faiths living together sometimes in harmony and sometimes in violent discord.

Historians disagree about the extent to which the British prioritized the security of their Indian empire in foreign policy decisions around the globe, particularly in Africa. We do know that the British were so concerned about maintaining their hold on India that much of their strategy revolved around keeping the frontiers of India safe from incursions and the route to India safe from interruption. British politicians constantly feared Russia to the north. Palmerston particularly wanted to reform the Ottoman empire that straddled the Middle East between Western Europe and Persia. A reformed Ottoman empire would mean a strong land power to keep the Russians and others out of the Middle East, which happened to be the main route for trade, supplies and troops to and from India. It was in this context—and because of the security concerns over India—that Britain found itself involved in a war against Russia.

The People's Darling

Much of Palmerston's popularity was due to the fact that he protected and extended the prestige of Britain as a great imperial power. Despite the tremendous influence Palmerston had, typical of British politics, he rotated in and out of the government a number of times before serving as prime minister. This is because his tenure at the Foreign Office did not flow smoothly. He came into office in 1830 as foreign secretary when Lord Grey became prime minister. Then Parliament dissolved and the Conservatives took power, throwing Palmerston out of office in 1841. From 1841 to 1846 he sat as a member of the opposition. In 1846, after the repeal of the Corn Laws, he returned to office as foreign secretary under Lord John Russell, occupied with the issue of the "Spanish Marriages," the Don Pacifico case, and the revolutions of 1848 that swept across Europe. Then when he approved a coup d'etat by Napoleon III, he angered many members of Parliament and his colleagues in the cabinet. At the request of the queen, who had grown tired of his independence and his refusal to consult her before first sending out dispatches, Lord John Russell dismissed him in 1851. He returned to the cabinet as minister for the Home Office in 1853, resigned, and then returned to office again in 1853, where he stayed until elected prime minister in 1855.

While in the opposition from 1841 to 1846 he blasted the foreign policy of Lord Aberdeen—the foreign secretary in the administration of Robert Peel. Unkindly, Palmerston ridiculed him as "an imbecile." Palmerston had reason to be jealous of him. Many in Parliament preferred Aberdeen because of his mild manners and his collaborative approach to colleagues in cabinet meetings. This made him appear a far more reasonable and responsible foreign secretary and provided a nice break for members of Parliament who had grown weary of Palmerston's mercurial temper.

National domestic issues also occupied his time, and these intimately related to his official position. He debated the abolition of the Corn Laws, voting as a Whig for the triumph of free trade. As usual, he roundly condemned the evils of slavery and preached for the use of the Royal Navy to abolish it on the high seas wherever found. He enthusiastically supported the Mines and Collieries Bill that reduced the work hours of children laboring under inhuman condition in the mines.

Being out of office gave him a chance to catch up on personal business. He visited a slate quarry that he partially owned in Wales, revisited his estates in Ireland, and spent more time at his home, Broadlands. *Punch* magazine poked fun at him in a cartoon captioned "Cupid Out of Place" and showing him sitting by the fire at home. He kept busy. But he did not remain peaceful for he itched to again take up the reins of foreign policy. Perhaps that explains why he lambasted Lord Aberdeen, his replacement, so mercilessly. He protested that Aberdeen and the current government led Britain into national decline, "sliding downwards by a very decently rapid Descent." In these years of opposition, too, the potato crop in Ireland led to disaster for the Irish population and pushed the issue of the Corn Laws to the forefront of national policy. The Conservative government led by Peel recommended repeal of the Corn Laws to howls of betrayal by landowning Tories who depended upon the government keeping the price of food—and thus their rent—high. But Peel lost the support of his own party over the issue and the Whigs again had their chance at government.

Some called for putting Palmerston back in at the Foreign Office. The new Whig prime minister, Lord Russell, attempted to form a ministry but explained to Palmerston the opposition of the radicals to his taking back the reins of foreign policy. He offered him instead the Colonial Office. When Palmerston refused, Russell then as a last resort offered him—reluctantly—the Foreign Office again. But Lord Grey, a powerful Whig who disagreed with his policies, refused to join the ministry with Palmerston in the Cabinet, and so the queen called the Tory Sir Robert Peel back to office. But Palmerston had merely to watch the rebellious Tories with Disraeli in the lead tear their own gifted leader, Robert Peel, into pieces. Once again Lord Russell attempted to form a government, and this time he succeeded. Lord Grey preferred holding office and so overcame his objections to Palmerston, and once again "Protocol Palmerston" was back in the saddle as foreign secretary.

Queen Victoria had strong and complex opinions on Palmerston. At first she liked him very much. When she became queen he carefully explained to her the intricacies of foreign policy and the issues involved with Russia, France, and Turkey. He introduced diplomats to her, wrote her careful and fatherly notes on how the young queen ought to address an ambassador from the Ottoman empire or an ambassador from the court at St. Petersburg. She found him pleasant, funny, and highly amusing, looking up to him as to a kindly uncle, riding with him in Windsor Great Park, playing chess with him, and visiting the seashore at Brighton with him in her entourage. This happy state of affairs lasted until her marriage to Albert.

But after her marriage she entrusted most of her counsels to her husband, who saw the world in very different terms from Lord Palmerston. The foreign secretary leaned too far toward constitutional government, sympathizing often with liberation movements in Europe and radicals at home. Palmerston pressed Russia and Austria hard to make concessions in the Middle East and favored republican France to the irritation of Prince Albert, who espoused a far more elevated view of monarchy and of the aristocratic role in the affairs of state. These issues were bound to come to a head and led eventually to a demand by the queen in December 1851 that he resign.

Disagreement in foreign policy issues exacerbated other more personal incidents that sabotaged his relationship with the queen. While she forced his resignation in 1851, she never forgave him for an incident that occurred in 1840 that would forever change her opinion of Palmerston as a gentleman. While staying the night in Windsor Castle he had broken into the bedroom of one of the queen's young maids, moved furniture to block all possible exits, and then attempted to force her into sex. She fought back, screaming loudly, and only the intervention of other guests saved her from rape. The queen banned him for some time from Windsor and, leaning toward the counsels of her handsome and morally severe husband, never again allowed herself to enthuse over Lord Palmerston. She also objected to his practice of sending out dispatches without always sending them for correction to her first, which resulted in a seesaw of complaints between them and excuses on his part never resolved until his resignation as foreign secretary in 1851.

Real tensions separated the queen and Palmerston. Palmerston had the ethics of the eighteenth century. Gentlemen from the eighteenth century did not approve of rape but certainly felt that the role of the man lay in forcing sexual attentions, loading women with compliments, and expecting her to resist if she could. Even by these standards Palmerston conducted himself in an ungentlemanly manner. The upper class sometimes—by no means always— took it for granted that it could use a lower-class maid as it wished. But Queen Victoria represented the ethics of a new age, one highly influenced by evangelical middle-class ethics and the protection of women as sacred. His actions in the palace that night appalled her, and in her view this made him unfit to hold office. Additionally, though he sincerely supported a constitutional monarchy in the English mold, his leanings toward liberalism and his tactical support of liberal revolution overseas made him at times appear to conservatives as a republican. Therefore it often seemed to the queen that his refusal to send all dispatches to her first were an almost deliberate insult to the monarchy. For his part, Palmerston felt that representative government should not be required to submit to the monarchy the details of foreign policy—that as a representative of the people he had the right to act in their interest—to inform the queen, yes—

to obey the dictates of her aristocratic and German husband—no. And as to his misconduct in the palace, he apologized—quite enough for an eighteenth-century man but not quite enough for Queen Victoria.

When Aberdeen formed a ministry, he needed Palmerston's support and the followers in Parliament he would bring with him. But the queen did not want Palmerston back at the Foreign Office, and so Aberdeen offered him a stint in the Home Office. Most accounts of Palmerston's life so focus on his time in the Foreign Office and as prime minister that his work as Home Secretary gets lost in the shuffle. But this period of his career is notable for a number of reasons. It shows how a powerful reform impulse set him aside distinctly from the Conservative Party, and it showcases his remarkably modern ideas, such as his successful efforts to reform the prison system and institute environmental reforms. These highly progressive efforts must balance our view of the man who also resisted reform of the electoral system and who was in many ways an odd mix of conservatism and reformist—not a moderate or a compromise between the two parties but a mix of impulses and ideas that appealed to the core constituency of each and may be the secret of his remarkable popularity.

He entered his new duties as Home Secretary cheerfully. He claimed in a letter to his brother, William, that he did not miss the nonstop work of the Foreign Office and rather enjoyed focusing on mere domestic issues. Perhaps he really meant his words, because he surprised almost everyone with the boundless energy he brought to his new job. He personally visited Parkhurst Prison on the Isle of Wight, where boys waited for transportation to Australia. The authorities ran the prison on military lines and housed over a hundred boys in small cells, hammocks hooked into the brick walls and a single desk with a Bible and candle for furniture. This Spartan environment seemed a vast improvement over chaining the boys inside the rotting hulls of retired sailing ships that still held many adult prisoners and where disease and violence wreaked havoc on the bodies and minds of the inmates. When Australia refused any further transport of convicts into their colony the prison population at Parkhurst and elsewhere threatened to balloon out of control. Palmerston solved this problem by pushing through Parliament a bill that allowed for "tickets of leave," or what is today called parole, a practice pioneered by Australia on Norfolk Island and in Ireland and introduced for the first time into Britain.

He worked closely with his evangelical friend, the famous reformer of social ills Anthony Ashely, Lord Shaftesbury, and introduced measures for the reform of factory law. In this regard he considered himself strictly a moderate, trying to balance the demands of factory owners with the advice of experts and workers. He introduced the Factory Act of 1853, which had the effect of limiting the hours of children and women to ten and a half hours per day. He drafted legislation that made the organization of unions legal and that forbade employers from paying workers in goods instead of cash—a clear abuse when employers priced the goods in their own factory stores and then doled them out as "pay." Other reforms followed that owe their origin to him and that sound distinctly modern. He proposed and passed the Smoke Abatement Bill that attempted to deal with the burgeoning pollution produced by burning coal, from steamers on the Thames to factories. While this legislation slowed down the accumulation of soot, the spreading Industrial Revolution only made it worse as the century wore on. It is remarkable as legislation, however, because it stands out as very early environmental action—using the government, in spite of support for free trade, to enforce rules for the good of the public health.

The Crimean War

While Palmerston worked hard on domestic issues, it is clear that his heart still lay in foreign policy. The advent of the Crimean War brought his foreign policy counsel back into play with the advice that he gave the prime minister, Lord Aberdeen. Palmerston argued forcefully to Aberdeen that Britain needed to protect the Ottoman empire against incursions by Russia, in order to protect British prestige as well as to secure the route to India. The papers of Palmerston and other cabinet members in the Aberdeen coalition show an overriding concern with Russia as a rival to British power and the need for Britain to show its muscle and intervene to stop the absolutist government of the czar from wresting land in Europe that had traditionally been ruled by the Ottomans.

Two forces joined hands in opposition to the Russians: the radicals and the newspapers. The radicals hated Russia for obvious reasons. The czar and his court, backed by a large landed class of aristocrats, ruled Russia. The Russian court represented everything the radicals hated—deeply held religious values, feudal relationships that emphasized hierarchy and the importance of birth, that is blood and breeding, in social relationships, and the traditional power and military ethics of the landed class and the throne. Russia aggravated this ideological cleavage by brutally repressing the rising middle classes in Poland who rebelled against Russian power in a vain attempt to establish a democratic government. This repression by the Russians raised howls of indignation throughout radical circles in Western Europe.

No one howled as loudly as the press. The mass-circulation newspapers played an increasingly large role in shaping public opinion, to such a point that it is fair to say that published opinion was indistinguishable from public opinion. The radicals of Europe had the strongest activist strain. The radicals represented many of the rising middle class, and they demanded their own newspapers. Businessmen gladly obliged and launched thousands of small dailies across Europe to meet the demands of this new market. Advertisers, mostly retailers and manufacturers of consumer items like Pears soap and Cadbury chocolates, added money to the income from subscription rates. The *Times* tended to be conservative, but most of the other dailies had strong radical strains and on the whole supported Palmerston. One paper, the *Morning Advertiser,* had wide circulation in the pubs, and Palmerston's punchy and aggressive statements made in Parliament gave him wide appeal in this growing middle-class market.

The constellation of power relations shifted in an unfortunate direction preceding the Crimean War and, with the press howling for blood, added to the difficulty of keeping the European Concert going. One of the events that set the stage for conflict occurred between France and Russia. Napoleon III in December of 1851 assumed dictatorial powers in France and proceeded to alienate the Russian czar by treating the czar as an equal. Russia and France also quarreled over which had responsibility to maintain the holy places in Palestine. This in turn put the Sultan in the uncomfortable position of pleasing—and failing to please—the conflicting claims of France and Russia. Frustrated with the lack of progress on the issue and determined to claim her hereditary rights as protector of the Christians—particularly of the Orthodox church within the Ottoman empire—the Russians claimed a protectorate over the holy places within the Ottoman empire. In addition, the czar proposed to the British that they jointly divide the Ottoman empire into spheres of influence, because the "sick man of Europe" was clearly dying and would not, the czar believed, last much longer.

The British ambassador to the Ottoman court agreed that the Ottoman empire teetered on the brink of total collapse. Britain, however, turned down the request for a secret agreement to carve up the Ottoman empire. Palmerston and the ambassador to the Porte, Stratford Canning, feared a general European war if the great powers fought over the pieces of the empire. The British had considerable influence on the Sultan, not least because the Sultan firmly believed that his only protection against Russian and Austrian aggression lay in the protection of the British fleet and army. Palmerston's anti-Russian attitude, by this time well developed, aided the Sultan's confidence in Britain. Palmerston argued against the Russian claims as sole protector of Christians in the Ottoman empire by making the point that more "security of persons and property" was given to Christians in the Ottoman empire than in Russia.

In response to the tensions over the holy places, the Russians threatened to move into Moldavia and Walachia, and Britain and France responded by sailing their fleets to the Golden Horn, the great port of Constantinople. A general of the Sultan, Omar Pasha, crossed the Danube River with his armies and faced the Russian forces in Moldavia and Walachia, with minor skirmishes that ran the risk of breaking out into a broader war. Then a Turkish fleet sailed into the Black Sea and Russia in return swiftly sank it. War was imminent, with France and Britain backing the Ottoman Empire on one side, and Russia on the other.

At this point, two camps existed in Britain. The prime minister, Lord Aberdeen, believed that the Russian Czar, Nicholas, sincerely professed his desire for peace with the Ottomans and believed the integrity of his intention to "internationalize" Constantinople and other European pieces of the Ottoman empire. Aberdeen agreed with Nicholas that Turkey had no hope of renewal from within. Palmerston on the other hand, distrusted the intentions of Russia, and forecast with optimism the possibilities of a reformed Ottoman empire. While Home Secretary and officially focused on domestic issues, Palmerston still exerted great influence in the cabinet on foreign affairs. Lord John Russell, the foreign secretary, found himself practically immobilized between the two polar positions.

Public opinion drove all these leaders, the Sultan, the czar, the British cabinet, and the politicians throughout Europe, making compromise difficult in the pursuit of peace. Russian newspapers highlighted the atrocities suffered by Christians under the autocratic Turkish regime and called loudly for the capture of the ancient capital of the Orthodox faith, Constantinople. The Sultan's subjects likewise shared a loathing of Russia and wanted no more concessions of territories or privileges to the northern giant. With the loss of Greece and other European enclaves the Turks believed they had lost too much prestige and been insulted beyond endurance. Europeans and Britons in particular suffered from the propaganda lash of the newspapers. The press had been viciously anti-Turkish when Lord Byron sailed to Greece to fight for independence against the Ottomans. Now the newspapers in Britain, only a few decades later, painted the czar as a power-hungry wolf devouring the Mediterranean for empire and a deadly threat to British trade and security. The press in Britain lavished praise on the once-reviled Ottoman empire and urged politicians to stand up to Russia and back the integrity of the Sultan's dominions.

These sentiments lay behind the Crimean War. Prominent poets shared the enthusiasm for war. Tennyson described the prospect of war with Russia as an opportunity for cleansing and for renewing manliness. He wrote of the coming conflict, that Britain will see "the sudden making of splendid names, and noble thought be freer under the sun." Palmerston wrote to a correspondent that the Russian government always took actions that would "push forward its encroachments as fast and as far as the apathy or want of firmness of other Governments would allow it to go, but always to stop and retire when it was met with decided resistance." One newspaper noted that the great Palmerston, as an old man now, stood up to the Russian bear as he had stood up as a boy to bullies at Harrow. Such encouragement was hard for Palmerston to resist, for he had always been sensitive to the pulse of public, and published, opinion.

While newspapers called loudly for war and must share the blame of the suffering that ensued, it is also true that war probably could have been averted if Palmerston, with his hard line, had been foreign secretary, and the rhetoric of Cobden, Bright, and other radicals who wanted at all cost to avoid war had not encouraged the Russians to believe that Britain would do little if they took more territory. Both the Russians and the French tended to be unstable diplomats during this period, and the British, in comparison, a steady hand. But Aberdeen made a series of tactical errors that clearly worsened the prewar situation and lurched from crisis to crisis. He told Madame Lieven, the wife of the Russian ambassador, that war would be an "act of insanity" and "utterly disgraceful." These confidences to Lieven of course made their way back to Russia and encouraged them all the more to act aggressively. Aberdeen and his ambassador to the Porte, Strafford Canning, also gave to the Sultan the impression that no matter how he resisted European-brokered compromises, the British would at all costs protect Constantinople from the Russians.

With this confidence the Sultan declared war on Russia. Even as Strafford Canning worked feverishly for peace the Turks sailed their ill-fated fleet into the calm waters of the Black Sea. After the Russian victory, the press exploded, running headlines in Britain calling the naval action a "massacre." Aberdeen, the papers screamed, had betrayed the British people to the Russian bear by not even putting up a fight; He was not only senile and incompetent, he was a coward.

Palmerston had sat by and watched the events, powerless to prevent them. With Aberdeen unwilling to follow his advice in the handling of the Russian advances, and with Aberdeen sinking in the public eye, lacerated by the newspapers that were the bedrock of his own popularity, Palmerston cut the tether that held him to the cabinet as Home Secretary and resigned. Authentic political conscience did play a role in the decision, however practical and self-serving his actions appear. The reform bill controversy raged at the same time, and he used differences over the bill with Aberdeen to step outside a government sinking almost as fast as had the Turkish fleet.

Meanwhile the war moved forward. Spooked by the calls for action and the personal attack on his character, Aberdeen decided to hammer out a plan with the French to protect Turkey, jointly sailing naval ships to Sebastopol, a Russian port city strategically located on the tip of a peninsula. The Russians, stung by the threat of naval action, recalled their ambassadors from Paris and London. Britain and France publicly announced their alliance with the Sultan, and a few weeks later fighting broke out.

But things went badly, since the British had had little experience fighting major wars for a generation, and the lessons of strategy and supply had to be learned in a new age under new conditions. Sending a thirty-thousand-man army fully equipped thousands of miles away from home proved daunting. In 1854 a storm sunk a convoy of supply ships. Food, clothing, even basics such as tents and ammunition ran perilously low, leaving soldiers exposed to bad winter weather and weakened to the point where thousands succumbed to the ravages of cholera. Florence Nightingale fought a stubborn and inefficient bureaucracy to provide basic and competent medical care for the soldiers. Worse, for Aberdeen, reporters narrated to the horrified reading public back home all the difficulties and all the horrors of what appeared to be an unsuccessful war effort.

Strategic errors by the generals did not help public support. Lord Raglan, a veteran soldier from the Battle of Waterloo in 1815, landed with British troops on the peninsula and attempted to dislodge the Russians before more reinforcements arrived. Above the British army on a wooded ridge the Russians formed a thin line of defense. The British gallantly crossed over a stream and fought uphill with sixty thousand troops to gain the ridge and in the process lost thirty-three hundred soldiers. The Russians lost eighteen hundred. If Raglan had followed up on his costly win by chasing down the fleeing Russian troops and then besieging Sevastopol—with the British navy assaulting by sea—he could have taken the city and ended the war early in triumph. But Raglan rested his troops. The Russians under the capable General Menshikoff made a bold, calculating stroke. The Russian fleet lay vulnerable in the port, unable to stand up to the better built, better equipped, and better trained British navy. So in a move that rivals Cortez burning his own fleet off the coast of Mexico, Menshikoff sank his own vessels, the hulls of the Russian ships blocking the harbor effectively. Now the might of the British navy could not be brought to bear on the siege of the northern part of the city, which lay north of the bay. The battle shifted almost entirely to a land-based engagement in the south, playing clearly on Russian, not British and French, strengths.

A secret intelligence source from inside Russia led the British to believe the city lay practically undefended and that another tack, despite Raglan's delay, would quickly force the Russian army to capitulate. This led to another disastrous result. Because the Aberdeen cabinet ordered little preparation for a long winter siege, the troops were undersupplied. The Russians in the meantime fortified the city and built up troop strength to one hundred thousand men. When the British finally charged the wall of the city the resulting skirmishes were disastrous. Using the eighteenth-century technique of bold cavalry charges into the face of artillery, Lord Cardigan led the famous Light Cavalry Brigade, immortalized by Tennyson as the "Charge of the Light Brigade." This attack, while showing incredible bravery, decimated the ranks and gained little strategic advantage.

The war losses appalled the British newspapers—the high death toll, the suffering of the troops, the lack of organization, the poor hospital facilities, the strategic blunders. The public had had enough of the failures. It wanted change. Lord John Russell resigned in January 1855 when he learned that Parliament intended to form a committee of inquiry on the war. When the House proceeded to vote for the inquiry 305 to 148, it meant that Lord Aberdeen lost the confidence of the house and he promptly tendered his resignation. Public opinion during this time had been turning toward Palmerston, dubbed "the inevitable," because the public saw him as forceful, unflappable, and decisive in foreign policy.

The queen still did not like him. But she had to call new ministers into office and so first turned to the conservative party leader Lord Derby to form a government. She claimed that Palmerston was too old for the job, that his day had gone by. But Derby could not pull together a majority, and the queen reluctantly and under pressure from the public at last turned to Palmerston to be the next prime minister of Britain.

Prime Minister

Calling Lord Palmerston to the premiership was a difficult pill for Queen Victoria to swallow. She had not completely forgiven him for his bad behavior in the palace, nor for his years of passive subversiveness in the Foreign Office, ignoring her advice and refusing to get her prior permission for all his actions and dispatches. But her attitude towards him in the meantime had somewhat mellowed. He had been invited to Balmoral Castle, the Scottish country residence of the royal family, and behaved himself with proper decorum. His work as Home Secretary did not conflict with the queen or Albert the way foreign policy did, and advocates of Palmerston were careful to credit him with being a changed man, a more sensitive and decorous man than he used to be. Victoria appeared to be softened by these suggestions. Palmerston became prime minister in February 1855. He was seventy-one years old.

The Aberdeen administration should not be remembered only for its mistakes in the Crimean War. It has many accomplishments to its record. This administration reformed and improved the relationship with Canada, halted the transportation of convicts to Australia, and opened the Civil Service in India to competition and merit—all accomplishments of note. A talented politician in the Cabinet, William Gladstone, proposed a bold and progressive budget that broadened the tax base while lowering the rates and lowering and abolishing a number of customs duties. These accomplishments all tend to be forgotten however in light of the mistakes made during the course of the Crimean War.

Palmerston swept into office with a mandate to win the war. He did not face office without opposition, however. Many predicted his new ministry would not stand. The Peelites in his coalition followed the pragmatic and reformist ideas of their old conservative leader, Robert Peel, and they objected to the parliamentary inquiry into the conduct of the war—because it implicated so many of their members. Palmerston failed despite his best efforts to persuade Parliament to abandon the committee of inquiry and was left holding the cabinet together without the crucial support of the Peelites. But his luck shifted. The *Times,* the most powerful and influential newspaper in Britain, threw its support behind Palmerston. Usually a critic of his foreign policy, due primarily to his support for liberal causes overseas, the *Times* understood that in Aberdeen's cabinet Palmerston had advocated a tough and decisive response to the Russians, which the newspaper liked. Parliament threw support behind the new prime minister precisely in order to win the Crimean War, and the paper saw in Palmerston the kind of warrior they wanted to carry the war through. Thus the most powerful and widely read paper in Britain became a propaganda ally—an incalculable boon.

His long years of experience at the war office now came into play. He immediately drew up a "memorandum of means" that listed the changes in war policy. He clarified the chain of command, the procurement process for the supply of the troops, and drastically cut through red tape, specifically the steps necessary to gain the permissions to carry out the "memorandum of means." The army rushed supplies to the troops, and proper roads—begun before Palmerston became premier—were completed from the port to the camp where the army lay outside the city of Sebastopol. The prime minister also fully backed the reforms of Florence Nightingale, who was a personal friend. She instituted vastly improved sanitary conditions for the soldiers and lowered the death toll, making her immensely popular with the public and securing her place in history as a pioneer of the nursing profession. And with better weather in the spring, the army began to look far more credible and professional, gaining the strategic points necessary to extract a heavy toll from the enemy. The progress against the Russians holed up in Sevastopol began to look so promising that the prospects for peace and a negotiated deal improved dramatically. In November 1854, Czar Nicholas ordered his ministers to compromise, and in March 1855 a new conference of the major European powers convened. Palmerston sent Lord John Russell to represent Britain in Vienna.

But the war did not resolve quickly despite these efforts. The Russian czar died in St. Petersburg, and the Vienna conference could not reach agreement. But with Russia continuing to suffer reverses, losing the south bay of Sevastopol, the giant bear showed signs of wanting out of the conflict. The English public did want peace, but it wanted victory even more and hoped for the fruits of peace only after enough military glory had been won by the British on the ground. But the plot thickened with the French emperor, Napoleon III, vacillating between cutting a quick deal for peace and at other times using the continuing war to appeal to nationalist revolution across Europe. Austria also tried to mediate. Then at last Russia agreed to four points that the major European powers had agreed on, and an armistice was signed February 29, 1856, and soon after, on March 30, the Peace of Paris, a treaty guaranteeing the independence of the Ottoman empire. Russia agreed, with great reluctance, to (1) make the Black Sea neutral, that is free of warships, (2) the right of only small cruisers on the Black Sea, (3) accept the promise made by the Sultan that he would treat Christians equal with Muslims, and (4) open the Danube River for international trade. The agreement at the Congress of Paris was a bitter pill for Russia to swallow. In fact Russia or the Sultan violated most of the provisions within twenty years, and so many historians do not think the war had accomplished its goal or that it was worth the suffering and expense that it entailed. The war, however, cemented Palmerston's reputation and laid the foundation for a long and successful run as prime minister, assuring that the principles of his foreign policy that had already affected Britain and the world so much continued as a force for change.

The Anglo-Persian War of 1856

After the Crimean War Palmerston faced two quick wars in succession that left Britain dangerously overextended. The first war was rather minor but still based on the fear of the Russians. Russia had urged the Persians to ally with them against the British and the French in the Crimean War. The Persian prime minister, Sadr Azim, rejected the offer. Instead of war in the west, Persia opted for a conflict far closer to home and one that directly expanded its eastern border: it captured the ancient city of Herat. In 1856 the city occupied the western edge of Afghanistan and overlooked the border of Persia. Overrun by almost every major empire of the region in the last twenty-five hundred years, it boasted a citadel built by the Greeks during the invasion of Alexander the Great. Persia eyed the city with jealousy because in the eighteenth century the Safavid empire, which included most of what is today modern Iran, also included Herat.

Twice in the nineteenth century the Persians had tried to wrest the city back from Afghan overlords, only to fail due to British pressure. Palmerston wanted to keep Afghanistan as a secure buffer state protecting the northwestern edge of India, and the suspicion that the Russians held undue influence over the Qajar dynasty that occupied the throne of Persia made the British determined to keep Herat part of Afghanistan.

Herat also sat at the crossroads of trade routes—less important in the age of steam shipping but still an important strategic position. The city lay in a fertile valley that overlooked Persia in the west, with the mountains of Afghanistan and then India in the east and Russia to the north. When Persian troops seized the ancient city the governor-general of Bombay, under orders from Palmerston, sent in the British Indian army to reclaim it. This action alone illustrates the importance of India to Britain. The Indian army maintained British power far from the British homeland and could project armed forces anywhere in the region. Due to the losses of the first Afghan war, and wishing to avoid dangerous travel for the army through the mountains of Afghanistan, the British fleet sailed into the Persian Gulf and took the port city of Bushire, and from there struck into the interior. A peace treaty was swiftly signed in Paris that restored Herat to Afghanistan. This conflict had hardly ended when the Indian Mutiny broke out and provided a far more serious challenge to British hegemony in the region.

The Indian Revolt

The most serious military threat to the British empire in the nineteenth century, after the defeat of Napoleon, was the mutiny of Indian soldiers in 1857. This war is called the Indian Mutiny by the British and often referred to as the First War of Independence in India. The rebellion broke out among the Indian soldiers of the Indian army, called Sepoys, who were trained and officered by the British. The army had issued a new rifle, the Enfield rifle, which required new cartridges. The cartridges were encased in a cardboard wrapping that held the black powder inside. The soldier had to tear the cartridge open with his teeth, empty the powder into the end of the musket, then push in the cardboard with a rod, ram the cardboard and the powder tight, then ram a lead musket ball down the barrel, and finally add a percussion cap before firing the rifle. All this was second nature to the soldiers.

But when word reached the Sepoys that the cartridges in the Calcutta factory were coated with beef tallow or pig fat, it offended and alarmed both the Hindu and Muslim soldiers. To place the fat of cows, for the Hindus, or the fat of pigs, for the Muslims, into their mouths, meant a serious violation of their faith—loss of caste for the Hindus and a grave sin for Muslims. The British had not actually distributed the cartridges yet and the factory officials caught the mistake before the army distributed the cartridges. But the damage had been done—rumor and speculation raged among the Sepoys that the British intended purposely to violate their faith in order to spread Christianity. This rumor fit the big picture of other rumors part and parcel with resistance to the British presence: railways and telegraph lines were large chains intended to hold down India and enslave India forever, the Sepoys were given new rifles because the British intended them to conquer Paris and China for them. They would all have to become Christians, eat beef and pork, and drink beer like English soldiers.

The first unrest occurred near Calcutta, at Barrackpur, which had four regiments with no British officers. Then the riots spread from Banares, Allahabad, Agra, Delhi, and Meerut, and finally on May 3, to Lucknow. At one fort a handful of British soldiers held out against thousands of Sepoys and then, ammunition exhausted, in a last desperate act blew themselves up and fifteen hundred attacking Sepoys with them. Throughout northern India British officers were killed and thousands of women and children mercilessly slaughtered. The rebels took over Delhi and proclaimed Bahadur Shah the new Mughal emperor of India. But with the help of those regiments made up of British soldiers, and Sikh soldiers who had remained true to the British cause, and other loyal Indians, the British wrestled Delhi back into their hands, relieved Lucknow and the other besieged cities, and reestablished their rule. The massacre of women and children so enraged the British soldiers that they punished hundreds of the rebels with the firing squad, even tying some rebels to the mussel of cannon and blowing them to pieces as a lesson that the massacre of women and children would be met with ferocity. The British response has been criticized as excessive, and critics at the time claimed that it exhibited the same callous disregard for life as the actions of the rebels.

No one ideological motive or political strategy caused the rebellion. Moneylenders, both British and Indian, were highly resented; the land tax hit the large landowners hard; and certainly racial insults abounded. But the single greatest cause was a sense of inequity. One Indian author, Sir Sayyid Ahmed Kahn, expressed this sentiment in 1859 when he wrote, "The natives of India, without perhaps a single exception, blame the Government for having deprived them of their position and dignity and for keeping them down." Many Indians resented the presence of an alien power and wanted independence because they shared the values of their colonial masters—a love of personal, and political liberty. This too often went unnoticed in Britain however, where the press had succeeded in whipping the public into a frenzy of revenge.

The Mosquito

While Victorians exhibited great alarm over the Indian rebellion, many conflicts that seem small in comparison may have engendered the greatest risk. The conflict over the Mosquito Coast, though often considered minor, is one such example. Palmerston felt successful in keeping the influence of Russia and France at bay, but less so regarding the United States. Russia had just lost the Crimean War; France was tied to British interests as an ally. But the United States continued to exert influence in Latin America and threatened to become a world power that could rival Britain in many parts of the globe. One small conflict in particular, that of the Mosquito Indian tribe on the coast of Central America, threatened to bring about a serious conflict between the United States and Britain. While Britain may have prevailed against the United States at sea, the impact on trade and the possibility of a land war over Canada presented an almost nightmarish challenge that would have certainly hurt Britain as a great power.

The Mosquito Coast ran along most of the coastline of what are today Nicaragua and a southern section of Honduras. It was inhabited by the Miskito Indians and its first European visitor was Christopher Columbus. The area had long been of interest to Britain because of an early attempt to settle a colony in the region by Puritans, and because in the sixteenth and seventeenth centuries buccaneers used the region as a staging ground for raids on Spanish galleons; later, pirates infested the ports. The inhabitants had a small European class of traders, and the Indians were a mix between black slaves and the original Indian tribes. Britain held the area as a protectorate between 1655 and 1850. When, in 1848, with the support of Britain, the Mosquito Indians seized Greytown, there a risk of war again arose, this time with the United States. The Indians and the largely white inhabitants of Nicaragua fought over the port of Greytown—what the Spanish called San Juan del Norte. The Clayton-Bulwer Treaty of 1850 settled this conflict, protecting the independence of the Mosquito Coast, and both the United States and Britain pledged not to colonize the area.

In 1859 Britain assigned its protectorate in the Mosquito Coast to the state of Honduras. While this relieved Britain of responsibility in the area, it displeased the Indians, who felt that the Honduran state would not treat them fairly. This led to a revolt by the Indians, but another treaty, in 1860, with Nicaragua, and giving to that country most of the area, including Greytown, settled tensions in the region. But now the United States feared that Britain would use its influence over the Nicaraguans to build a canal linking the Pacific and Atlantic Ocean and thus control the vital trade that now went around the horn of South America.

Into this volatile mix of unhappy parties came William Walker, a journalist from San Francisco. After attempting unsuccessfully to conquer with a handful of adventurers Lower California from the Mexican government, liberal sympathizers in Nicaragua invited Walker to set up a government there. This he did, with visionary Americans who joined him in his raid, and with the support of locals who wished for closer ties to the United States and who even dreamed of attaining American statehood. The United States government recognized, and even welcomed, this new regime.

Walker intended to reintroduce slavery in the region, and in 1856 he conquered Greytown as a new base for the importation of slaves. But Palmerston, whom as noted burned with anger at the issue of slavery, was furious at the action. He called his cabinet together and proposed an immediate blockade. But the cooler head of Clarendon, the foreign secretary, whom Palmerston highly respected, prevailed. War with the United States, a growing titan, would be disastrous for all concerned. The navy, Clarendon suggested, should be sent to Greytown to send a message, but no action should be taken until negotiations were given a chance. Prince Albert, Victoria's husband, also played a role, by toning down the dispatch that Palmerston sent to the president of the United States. To all these changes Palmerston reluctantly agreed. Fortunately for both powers, the United States backed down in the dispute and the United States then also withdrew support for Walker, and a devastating war between the two powers was averted. A few years later the British captured Walker at sea and handed him over as a prisoner to the Honduran government, which subsequently had him shot by a firing squad.

The *Arrow*

The struggle for influence with the United States in Latin America paralleled a struggle in the Far East with China. In the year before the Indian Mutiny, in 1856, the Chinese authorities intercepted a fast sailing vessel, called a lorcha, and arrested the crew. The name of the vessel was the *Arrow,* and the incident would lead to the fall of the Palmerston government, new elections, and his triumphant return. The incident also illustrates how the disagreement over opium created ill will on both sides of the issue, and how Britain, with Palmerston at her helm, had every intention of opening up this region of the world to trade and bringing China into the orbit of Britain's informal empire of economic exchange.

The Treaty of Nanking, signed in 1842 with Palmerston's support, opened trade with the West but still allowed China to forbid, internally, the use and sale of opium. The treaty also opened the door to western missionaries who began winning converts to Christianity and who, in agreement with the Chinese government, opposed the use of opium as a debilitating drug. Lord Shaftsbury often expressed to Palmerston the opposition of evangelicals, particularly missionary societies, to the British import of opium into China. But stronger forces were at play, and British merchants argued successfully that free trade ought to prevail. Merchants usually had Palmerston's ear, and he urged the Chinese government to legalize and then tax the use of opium. He took this line, since the Chinese government proved ineffectual at stopping either the domestic production of the drug or the smuggling of the drug through its porous coastline, and it seemed more sensible to regulate and profit from the drug than to ineffectually criminalize it.

The legal issues surrounding the *Arrow* affair are murky. Hong Kong, a British colonial port won from the Chinese in the 1842 Treaty of Nanking, had licensed vessels trading with the mainland of China. The Chinese captain of the *Arrow* lived in Hong Kong and flew the British flag on his boat and thus claimed British protection. But there can be little doubt that the Arrow smuggled contraband, including opium, into China. In hindsight many British officials saw the mistake of so freely licensing ships and allowing them to fly the Union Jack when engaged in illegal activity that included even such distasteful activities as piracy and the smuggling of "coolies" to Cuba and the West Indies.

But the incident with the *Arrow* placed Palmerston in a very difficult situation. He knew that the British demands in this case had not been entirely fair. But he also felt he had to demand the release of the vessel's crew and an apology because the prestige of Britain in that region of the world was on the line. Accordingly, when Parliament convened in 1857 it heard a speech from the throne, written by Palmerston, that stated all these conflicting interests in a simple and diplomatic demand to the Chinese government,

> Her Majesty commands us to inform you that acts of violence, insults to the British flag, and infraction of treaty rights committed by the local Chinese authorities at Canton, and a pertinacious refusal of redress, have rendered it necessary for Her Majesty's officers in China to have recourse to measures of force to obtain satisfaction. Those measures had, up to the date of the last accounts, been taken with great forbearance, but with signal success as regards the conflict to which they had led. We are commanded to inform you that Her Majesty trusts that the Government of Peking will see the propriety of affording the satisfaction demanded, and of faithfully fulfilling its treaty engagements.

When the Chinese released the crew but refused to apologize, the British navy then fired on (and destroyed) a number of forts on the Canton River. This only caused outrage in Parliament, among the radical wing, members such as Richard Cobden and John Bright, and less sincerely among the Conservatives, in an effort to force a vote of confidence and bring Palmerston's government down. The Conservatives with Disraeli at their helm taunted Palmerston to call an election and see just how much support he had. The radicals were even more severe and expected the electorate to give him a good beating, though others doubted this would be the case. But Palmerston seemed unshaken and sure of his ground. The queen wrote in her journal, "Lord Palmerston came at 6 . . . 'It was an old Whig notion,' Lord P. said, 'to resign in order to come in stronger!'"

When the vote of confidence arose and he lost, Palmerston, sure of his base, then dissolved the government and called for elections. Standing up to a corrupt foreign power, defending the right of free trade, and, above all, defending those under British protection to fly the British flag for peaceful purposes anywhere in the world, these were themes that appealed to the newspaper-reading electorate. As he hoped, the elections returned the Whigs stronger than ever.

The queen was ecstatic. She had slowly gained more respect for Palmerston, who treated her with every civility. She wrote that she was "glad to see that everything went off so well at Tiverton [Palmerston's own district] and that the elections are going on so famously. . . . That Messrs. Bright, M. Gibson, Cobden, and Layard, Sr., J. Walmsley, etc should be turned out, is excellent, and very striking."

Palmerston wrote to the queen,

> Viscount Palmerston presents his humble duty to your Majesty and has had the honour to receive your majesty's communication of yesterday. The result of the elections as far as they have gone is indeed highly satisfactory and the

calculation is that on the whole the Government will gain 40 seats, which would make a difference of 80 in a division.

With this increased backing Palmerston made a further demand on the Chinese emperor, the Son of Heaven. Because Britain had borne the cost and the responsibility of opening up China for not only itself but for other European powers and the United States, he determined to use the friction that arose at Canton as an opportunity to make China "grow up" and treat other nations as equals: He wanted the Chinese court to officially recognize the British and other European diplomatic delegations in Peking. Uniting with the French, British forces captured more forts on the Peiho River in 1858, and then, finally reaching the capital of Peking in 1860, the Chinese authorities gave way to the British demands. When twenty foreigners were murdered in revenge, the Europeans burned down the Summer Palace as a lesson to the authorities. These harsh conflicts finally accomplished what centuries of European requests did not: they opened China to the West and to a program of westernization and reform.

Marriage Law

Just as the Indian Mutiny broke out in northern India in 1857 another revolution occurred, of a different nature, in Britain. The Matrimonial Causes Bill stirred the pot of public opinion and exhibits a rather different Palmerston than normally seen in foreign affairs. The bill had been introduced with Palmerston's support in the House of Lords, where it passed, and then brought to the floor of the lower house, where it faced much domestic opposition, particularly from the clergy. This is a rare example of Palmerston facing down, rather than leading, public opinion. He waded through opposition and patiently guided the bill through the necessary steps to passage. The bill, while still not providing equal provisions for men and women in the case of a divorce, is seen by many to be a major step toward equality for women, and one of the first of a series of sexual reforms that Britain pioneered, and thus also one of the milestones in the history of equality between the sexes.

Previous to the bill the ecclesiastical courts granted divorces where the wife had committed adultery or the husband had been guilty of rape or abuse. Victorian society considered male adultery normal, if not moral. But this kind of divorce did not include the right of remarriage; rather, the parties were simply allowed to live separately. Men with a great deal of money could go one step further, however, and approach Parliament for a private bill that gave them a divorce that included the right to remarry. The Matrimonial Causes Bill (sometimes referred to as the 1857 Divorce Act) changed this, because it allowed the poor to get the same divorce that a private act of Parliament had only given rich men. In addition divorce proceedings moved out of the hands of the church and into the hands of the secular courts. Samuel Wilberforce, Bishop of Oxford, and Gladstone, a sternly evangelical member of the Church of England and a future Liberal prime minister, vociferously opposed the bill. Not only did the Bible condemn divorce, Gladstone thundered in Parliament, but it also condemned remarriage of divorced parties. Those who did remarry were living in sin, and such immoral actions should not be sanctioned or encouraged by the state.

Palmerston felt differently and argued that to forbid marriage to the guilty partners after a divorce simply encouraged people to live together without marriage. The bill in question advanced women's equality by the simple fact that under the law she was regarded as her husband's property, a legal entity submerged into his authority and person. Divorce meant that she regained the right to own her own property once more. She became, in effect, a legal entity once more.

The bill did not, however, treat men and women equally. The man could still get a divorce if his wife committed adultery even once. She could sue for divorce only if her husband had committed adultery repeatedly and in addition had been unusually cruel or deserted her entirely. Palmerston defended this provision as a concession to the generally held belief that it certainly was worse for a woman to commit adultery than a man. His own personal history of affairs must have influenced his judgment on this point.

The bill also made another kind of history. It sparked the beginning of the "filibuster," as it is called in the United States. Gladstone insisted to Palmerston that the bill would never pass. He and his colleagues would talk endlessly into the night until the other members who supported the bill simply gave up. But Palmerston, though in his seventies, kept the house sitting in the hot summer months and did not adjourn until the weary House voted on the issue. He watched over the progress of the debates carefully, listening to every speech, watching every turn in the debate, often into the early hours of the morning, showing more stamina than many of the young members of the House. The bill finally passed on August 25, 1857.

The passage of the bill is also noteworthy because even though women at this time could not vote, it marked one of the first major bills to pass Parliament because women lobbied politicians and appealed to public opinion. One woman in particular, Caroline Norton, proved decisive in bringing to the notice of the country how many women suffered under the old divorce laws. Norton had left her husband because of his violent abuse, and when he discovered that she had subsequently had an affair with the Whig prime minister, Lord Melbourne, he took custody of her children. She filed for divorce and tried to recover them. Lord Norton, her legal husband, objected to her attempt to gain divorce and custody of the children, and he won his case in court. Caroline Norton therefore lived unwillingly as Mrs. Norton for many years. She threw herself into the writing of pamphlets and novels that brought attention to these problems. Palmerston knew Caroline Norton and agreed with her advocacy for reform.

Popularity, Style, and the Liberal Party

Palmerston's popularity never rested on his reputation as a reformer. But his popularity extended beyond his aristocratic Whig base, and beyond the merchants and shopkeepers who made up the British "shopocracy," as detractors have called it. His support ran surprisingly deep among "the people," and, particularly after he became prime minister, among the working class.

After his death, his base of support splintered into different directions and sustained a popular style of leadership that Palmerston had pioneered, and that benefited both Liberals and Tories. Benjamin Disraeli inherited the mystique that came from wearing the mantle of imperial expansion, as did the Liberal imperialist Roseberry at the end of the nineteenth century. Gladstone inherited Palmerston's appeal to the common man. Some historians claim that David Lloyd George during the First World War had the "common touch" of Palmerston, though the connection seems rather tenuous given the latter era's distance from the mid-Victorian period. While it is easy to see how Palmerston's imperial policy was popular to all classes, historians have been baffled how Palmerston, who so adamantly opposed further elector reform, gained the support of precisely those middle- and working-class voters whose representation he opposed, particularly in the 1860s, when the agitation for reform picked up steam again.

Luck partially, but not completely, explains the secret of his popularity. Perhaps the largest pool of his popular support lay in a segment (not the whole) of the millions who had backed the Chartist movement. The movement spawned hundreds of small newspapers and mass meetings where the dynamic leadership of people like Cobden created an expectation in the public of a leadership of a particular sort—outspoken to the point of bluntness, masculine, gutsy, and unapologetically patriotic, all aimed at pleasing an audience of working- and middle-class citizens proud of an expanding economy and empire. They were proud also of Britain's role as arbiter of the peace, guardian of free trade, mistress of the sea, and mistress of a seaborne empire that straddled the continents with exotic and romantic ports of call ready for immigrants and teeming with opportunity. These supporters of the Chartist movement created a new body of public opinion among those determined to rise up in society and find their rightful place in the ever-expanding British world.

Palmerston's luck had something to with his successful navigation of the 1850s. First the 1832 reform bill had for a time quieted the agitation for yet more reform and satisfied the demand for further representation. When the Corn Laws were abolished 1846 and the final embers of the Chartist movement died down in 1848 the mass constituency that had backed these movements found no ready outlet for expression, and no single leader. Add to that an expanding and prosperous economy1850s when Palmerston first entered into office as prime minister in 1855, and he stood in line as heir apparent for this popular energy. If the demand for reform had still been alive, he could have inherited a government facing a whirlwind of instability and criticism. Instead he emerged with a broad base of support for a number of reasons, including his foreign policy and his style of leadership.

Issues of foreign policy punctuated the otherwise quiescent domestic landscape in the 1850s and provided Palmerston with precisely that theater of operation in which he so excelled. He could throw in concessions to the former Chartists without risking too much opposition from his aristocratic and manufacturing base. He refused in 1850, as Home Secretary, to prosecute workers at the Barclay and Perkins Brewery when they attacked a visiting Austrian general, Baron von Haynau. This general was known for his brutality in putting down Hungarian rebels in 1849, and for flogging Italian women in Brescia during an Italian revolt against Austrian rule. A Viennese refugee who worked as a clerk at the famous brewery recognized the general by his stupendous mustache, and sounded the alarm to other workers. They were familiar with his deeds due to the activities of the London street patterers—an impoverished band of newspaper hawkers that specialized in scandalous announcements. The workers roughed him up, pulled on his mustache, and then chased him with brooms out of the brewery, after which he hid in a local inn till rescued by police. This riot outraged not only the Austrian court but also Queen Victoria and Prince Albert. Palmerston's refusal to prosecute the brewery workers only added to the groundswell of support he enjoyed among workers throughout Britain. He also in 1851 had offered asylum to Lewis Kossuth, a hero of the democratic movement in Hungary, and supported pardons in 1854 for a number of political offenders in the Chartist cause. While no supporter of further reform, he had effectively become a hero of many reformers

Other hugely popular gestures followed. He publicly supported bands playing music in Hyde park on Sundays, and demanded that iron rails installed to keep people off the grass be removed. Parks, he said, were there precisely for people to walk in and enjoy. He also benefited from the perception that he had by his decisive leadership won and thus ended the Crimean War. He stood for free trade everywhere, even if the door of trade were kicked in by force, such as in the bombardment of China. His forward policy on imperial expansion was popular among all classes, even if opposed by many radicals. In this period his popularity soared, carrying over into his second and third election as prime minister. Even his sexual scandals may have added to his popularity, though this is very hard to judge. When just before his election in 1865 the husband of a Mrs. O'Kane sued him for thirty thousand pounds in court for seducing his wife. A ballad circulated celebrating his "Kiss."

All men throughout the nation will
Protect our old Premier,
And he always shall be guarded
By Britannia's Volunteers.
And suppose he kissed the covey's wife,
But proof cannot be found,
It ought to be a stunning kiss

For thirty thousand pounds.

The joke circulated that if she was "Cain," was he, at seventy-eight, "Able"? The assumption that Lord Cupid was still capable of scandalous behavior may well have added to his mystique among a working class that celebrated masculine prowess.

Certain things did cut against his popularity but did not materially erode the broad base of his support. In January 1858 an Italian nationalist threw a bomb at the French emperor, Napoleon III. The assassin missed his target but killed numerous bystanders and forced Palmerston across the Channel into an unexpected political ambush. Investigations by French police discovered that the bomb had been secretly manufactured in Britain, and that a group of revolutionaries who had gained asylum in Britain used London as their base to hatch their revolutionary schemes. It seemed reasonable to Palmerston to support an Aliens Act that would give his Secretary of State the power to expel foreigners who conspired to assassinate officials abroad. It also seemed reasonable to support such a bill to placate the French government.

The French press was not so easily mollified, however. Outraged headlines and editorials exclaimed that perfidious Albion, their old foe in battle, nourished assassins and revolutionaries in the bosom of London. This nest of vipers now hatched schemes to murder their own emperor. Had not the English also plotted the death of Napoleon on St. Helena, and stripped the republic of so much of its overseas empire?

The French outrage provoked the English press in turn. The French had always been bad losers and now they were insulting the honor of Britannia. A gaggle of French army colonels had petitioned Napoleon III to take rash action against the British, and this same weak despot now demanded that the sacred Parliament of a great and free people ban freedom of association and speech for foreigners.

In this sudden political squall, Palmerston faltered on the floor of the house, answering poorly, due perhaps as much to gout as to surprise and exhaustion. His timid answers were met with howls of indignation and mockery: he was a pawn in the game of high diplomacy that he had once mastered so well: he was, as the press implied, Bonaparte's jackal. The vote on the Aliens Act moved forward to the disquiet of his supporters and then went down in defeat. Then, to the surprise of almost everyone, he resigned his ministry.

He could still have stayed in office in this period, 1858–59, because few considered the bill to be of central importance. Many attributed this sudden resignation to an overweening pride. Perhaps Palmerston was insulted by the sudden and vicious attack and retreated from leadership to sulk and lick his wounds. But that was an unlikely explanation, given his inexplicable behavior out of office: he seemed as jolly and relaxed as ever; he attended Parliament punctually; he cracked jokes and engaged his colleagues cheerfully as if nothing had happened.

Meantime, he did not seem to lack popular support on the street. While Napoleon the III was unpopular among the radicals in parliament, the French emperor actually had a following among the lower classes in Britain. Irish laborers in Britain cheered his support for Catholicism. Napoleon III also represented, in the minds of many, the republican ideals of his forebearer, Napoleon, and attracted the admiration of a substantial cross section of working-class men who supported his uncompromising stance for Polish independence from Russia. Palmerston, therefore, while losing support in Parliament over this particular vote had not yet exhausted the deep reservoir of support held at large.

While his supporters called for his return to office, Palmerston patiently bided his time. He worked closely with a rival for the premiership, Lord John Russell, and pulled together a momentous meeting of Liberal supporters to hammer out a common party program. Gathering at the famous Almack's club, the disparate factions of the Liberal Party, so ready to fly apart and form unstable coalitions for their own advancement, came together. Later, when the queen called Palmerston back to office, he had behind him a unified party cemented together by a common program and a determination to hold and not lose power to the Conservatives. This alliance of interests served Palmerston, William Gladstone, and other Liberal party leaders for three decades.

His role in the unification of the Italian states cut both ways with his support among radicals and the working class. When Napoleon III aided Italian revolutionaries against Austria, the British government remained neutral. Palmerston, however, felt personally betrayed when he learned that Napoleon III gained the territory of Savoy and Nice in payment for this intervention. But events inside Italy swiftly changed the political topography. In 1860 the republican Garibaldi prepared to cross the Strait of Messina from Sicily into Italy with the express purpose of unifying the country and throwing off Austrian domination in the north. The French wished to stop the "redshirts" because the republicans did not support the Papal States. In response to this threat, the French government suggested a joint operation with the British navy in which the British and French fleets would patrol the Strait of Messina and keep the peace. Palmerston rejected the request. Instead he kept the British fleet close to the scene and allowed Garibaldi's army to pass—to the wild enthusiasm of the British public. Palmerston's critics were appalled at his popularity. One detractor quipped that never did one man get so much credit for doing so little. These postures overseas greatly aided Palmerston's popularity at home and detracted from his resistance to reform during his second term.

Civil War in the United States

On his return to office as prime minister in 1859, another crisis overseas distracted Palmerston and the newspaper-reading public from pressing domestic concerns. When civil war broke out between the northern and southern sections of the United States, public opinion in Britain also split into factions, some favoring the Union, others the Confederacy. Palmerston often thought that

American statesmen, whether from the northern or the southern states, were not gentlemen and lacked both education and breeding. He also felt that the tone of democratic politics in the United States produced dishonest demagogues rather than honest politicians. For this reason, and because he did not think a brokered peace between the North and the South would be in the interests of the American people, he preferred to keep Britain neutral during the conflict and not commit to one side or the other. But in November, 1862, Palmerston's cabinet gave serious consideration to the idea of siding with the American South. The idea—supported by Russell and Gladstone—was vigorously opposed by the other members of the Cabinet. Palmerston, after wavering, kept Britain on a neutral footing.

Regarding the American people, though, he held quite different feelings. The Americans were the cousins of the British, and the war between the North and South struck him and many British observers as "unnatural." He wrote to a friend in 1861,

> The danger is that, in the excited state of men's minds in America, the offer of anyone to interpose to arrest their action, and disappoint them of their expected triumph, might be resented by both sides; and that jealousy of European, especially of English, interference in their internal affairs might make them still more prone to reject our offer as impertinent.

He also could not see a solution that would please both sides. But others lobbied Palmerston to roll up his sleeves and broker a peace for practical reasons: Cotton supplied the lifeblood of the manufacturing districts that produced textiles sold around the world at great profit. At the heart of the empire of trade the textile factories pumped out bales of clothing that filled sailing and steam vessels that penetrated the vast and growing empire, formal and informal. This led Palmerston to write to the president of the British board of trade, Milner Gibson, asking for and giving advice. In this letter, also quoted at length by Palmerston's early biographer Evelyn Ashley, a number of issues that he raises tell us much about Britain and the empire of trade at this time.

First, though Palmerston is strongly against slavery, he is not much concerned about the issue in the United States, for it does not lead him to take a pro-northern stance. In addition, the letter emphasizes his true concern: economics. The supply of cotton to the manufacturers is vital, and he is much concerned about employment of the working class should the supply be cut off. Finally, he shows disdain for the business class of manufacturers. True to the ideals of his aristocratic class, he takes a longer view than just that of immediate profits, and is concerned about the future and the operation of trade far beyond one year's immediate profit. He also sees the empire as a source for the future supply of cotton, illustrating the global nature of his planning, and the utility of the entire empire to Britain's economy. He takes for granted substantial influence and trade from regions where the English have built no formal empire. He also views the issue of keeping the seas open from the aggression of the northern states as a very easy and doable operation if France should join Britain in the effort—a military assessment that seems quite correct given the naval capacity of the United States at the time.

My dear Milner Gibson—It is wise when the weather is fine to put one's house in wind and water-tight condition against the time when foul weather may come on. The reports from our manufacturing districts are at present good; the mills are all working, and the people are in full employment. But we must expect a change towards the end of next autumn, and during the winter and the spring of next year. The civil war in America must infallibly diminish to a great degree our supply of cotton, unless indeed, England and France should, as suggested by M. Mercier, the French Minister at Washington, compel the Northern States to let the cotton come to Europe from the South; but this would almost be tantamount to a war with the north, although not perhaps a very formable thing for England and France combined. But even then this year's crop must be less plentiful than that of last year. Well, then, has the Board of Trade, or has any other department of the Government, any means of procuring or of helping to procure anywhere in the wide world a subsidiary supply of cotton? As to our manufacturers themselves, they will do nothing unless directed and pushed on. They are some of the most helpless and shortsighted of men. They are like the people who held out their dishes and prayed that it might rain plum-puddings. They come of its own accord. They say they have for years been looking to India as a source of supply; but their looks seem to have had only the first effect of the eyes of the rattlesnake, vis., signs of falling into their jaws. The western coast of Africa, the eastern coast of Africa, India, Australia, the Fiji Islands, Syria, and Egypt, all grow great quantities of cotton, not to mention China, and probably Japan. If active measures were taken in time to draw from these places such quantities of cotton as might be procured, some portion at least of the probable falling off of this next year might be made good, and our demand this year would make a better supply spring up for the future years. I do not know whether you can do anything in the matter; but it is an important one, and deserves attention.

Certain events, however, pushed Britain close to war with the federal government in Washington, D.C. The British mail steamship the *Trent* carried on board two envoys, James Mason and John Slidell, from the Confederate states steaming from Cuba to England—Mason bound for London and Slidell to Paris. In November of 1861, cruising through the Bahama Channel, a strait off the northern coast of Cuba, an American warship, the *San Jacinto,* stopped the *Trent,* and on the command of Captain Charles Wilkes searched the crew and arrested Mason and Slidell. They were handed over to the federal government and promptly imprisoned in Boston at Fort Warren. This violation of national sovereignty could not be ignored. The arrests took place on a British vessel on the open sea and thus were highly illegal, made worse by the fact that the two men were diplomats who should have enjoyed special protection. The American government had long condemned acts such as this on the part of the British navy and so their action—and the vote of thanks to Captain Wilkes by the American

Congress—created outrage in Britain. In response, Palmerston sent an expedition of troops to Canada as a warning to the United States that Britain was prepared for war. It also showed the Americans that the British meant to protect their shipping against such incursions.

But Prince Albert and U.S. president Lincoln mitigated Palmerston's strong action, and both countries backed down from the brink of war. The husband of Queen Victoria suggested that the dispatch of protest from Britain to Washington include a face-saving clause that the British believed Captain Wilkes did not act on the advice of Washington but on his own. Lincoln as well wisely accepted this genteel suggestion that the whole affair had been a mistake, and, certain that war with the British would be a disaster, particularly given the help that the Confederates would then receive from their new ally, quickly patched up relations and released the two diplomats. It is hard to know if Palmerston's strong action laid the groundwork for a solution, or if he pushed the two countries unnecessarily toward war. His style of management in foreign affairs appeared often in this pattern: a tough initial response followed by moderation and compromise.

But another conflict with the Americans loomed, the affair of the *Alabama*. Confederate representatives commissioned a private ship to be built in a British port that could then be equipped at sea as a privateer for war, replete with cannon and other weapons. The Confederate states desperately needed to intercept the shipping of the North and build its navy to lift, partially at least, the embargo on their own ports that strangled the southern economy. The ships did not violate the British neutrality laws directly because they were built unarmed, with weapons to be added later. But Charles Adams, the ambassador from Washington to the court of St. James, objected to the contract. He had good reasons for doing so. The *Alabama,* along with the *Florida,* the *Georgia,* the *Rappahannock, and* the *Shenandoah,* sank 150 northern ships during the course of the war. The British government refused at first to intervene. The ships were lawfully contracted, and further, the British did not take sides between the North and the South, and much public sympathy lay with the right of the South to secede, the actions of the North appearing unconstitutional and brutal, despite the fact that the North took an antislavery position. But on further objections from Washington the British decided to give in to the demands. Not before, however, the *Alabama* managed to slip out of port and sail safely to the Confederate states, where at sea the ship received her cannons and then began her wildly successful service for the South, sinking fifty-eight northern merchant ships.

The fact is that the British tried to ignore the protests about the *Alabama.* William Gladstone in Parliament, a future prime minister, remarked with admiration that Jefferson Davis, the president of the Confederacy, had made an army, a navy, and now forged a new nation. This remark alerted the Washington government to the dangerously high level of support that the South enjoyed in Britain. The northern states assumed that a British government so opposed to slavery would clearly support the North against the slave-owning south. But

Washington had miscalculated. The United States pushed back the frontiers of its huge land empire yearly, and the nation's population and industrial wealth had swelled to leviathan proportions. Breaking the United States into two pieces removed the imminent prospect of a rising great power threatening Britain's status as the most powerful nation in the world. Also, the South had an aristocracy, like Britain, and this naturally led some in Britain to assume the South represented a check on the democratic mobs that ruled the American cities in the North. Should not the British aristocracy show support for their own class abroad and support the moderation and good breeding that accompanied this class? Further, the South provided cotton for Manchester textiles, and if the South were to become independent this would give Britain more support in the region and more influence, and, though the term was not used at the time, perhaps even an informal empire, a virtual colony, such as Britain enjoyed in parts of Latin America and Africa.

While Britain and the United States reached a number of compromises in this last period of Palmerston's life, the relationship between Britain and the United States soon changed. As the United States gained in population and wealth, it gained also in power. This forced Britain for the rest of the century to compromise more and pay far more attention to its cousin in the west. Additionally, in the 1860s and 1870s Europe began to catch up with Britain in economic power as the Industrial Revolution continued to spread throughout the northwest region of the continent. Russia gained in power, and no European entity increased more rapidly in the following decades than the quickly unifying states of Germany, with the awesome might of its advance in coal and steel production. Britain could not expect to go it alone forever. "Splendid Isolation," a term used to describe the British approach to the balance of power in Europe and the pursuit of interests abroad, continued to define the foreign policy approach for almost another thirty years. But by the end of the American Civil War, many began to wonder if Britain needed more allies to survive in a world where the British economy no longer dominated. In fact, even though Britain was busily "painting the map red" with the extension of its formal colonies, observers began to wonder if Britain's outward power concealed a growing inward weakness as it lost out in relative terms to its rivals.

5

Palmerston and the World Britannica

In the spring of 1865 the Civil War between the states had ended and Palmerston served his last year in office. But even as the American Civil War died down in the west, cold winds blew in from the east. Like boulders rumbling under the waves unseen, changes on the continent of Europe moved menacingly under the calm surface and, not for the last time, Britain took comfort in the great channel of cold Atlantic water that separated her from the gigantic land powers of Europe. In 1863 the Poles again rose in revolt against Russia. The French emperor, Napoleon III, asked Palmerston to call a new European Congress to settle the question. But Palmerston demurred—the Russians had laid the groundwork for their repression of the Poles by bringing Prussia to a secret understanding of support as an ally in case of war. Palmerston assumed that the French were using the opportunity to create war with Germany and recover territory on the Rhine. Palmerston may have correctly read the cards in this case, and it was not a pleasant reading—European powers grew yearly in economic might, including the size of their cities, transport, railways, and armaments. Every year Britain lost influence in Europe. Any future entanglements would prove far more costly to Britain in blood and treasure than conflicts of the past. "Old Pam," as the cartoons dubbed him, could no longer bluster his way through diplomatic difficulties with threats and gunboats.

At home his popularity made him unassailable, even when he did nothing to support the popular issue of electoral reform. When Lord John Russell, who had sponsored the first Reform bill twenty-nine years earlier, wished to sponsor another bill for further expanding the voting franchise, Palmerston gave only lukewarm support. Broadening the franchise, he feared, would merely give the vote of the great manufacturing towns to trade unions. It might also deny entrance into Parliament those wealthy and intelligent Whigs who brought with them so much talent. Fortunately for Palmerston, the idea of further reform did not at this time catch the public imagination. His campaign to fortify the coasts of England proved far more interesting to the newspaper-reading public, who largely agreed with Palmerston that France was not to be trusted, and that a "bridge of steam" could cross French troops into England on short notice. While this scenario proved illusionary, it also struck a chord with a public who felt that Britain had been caught unprepared by the Crimean War. Reform, clearly, would have to wait until Palmerston died. Gladstone, a strong advocate for reform, stood waiting in the wings.

Britain's Relative Decline of Power

Palmerston had to face in old age what he never had to face in middle age—the material increase of European power. The whole world was changing, and the absolute growth of Britain's trade and empire could not conceal the fact that Britain had to face a world where other great powers had begun to emerge. In "real politik" as practiced on the continent relative power equaled real power. When Bismarck seized the German-speaking territories of Sleswig and Holstein from Denmark, Palmerston at first played to the popular press at home by standing up to what he called the iron-heeled German bully in defense of the two helpless little Duchies. But this was not a pillow fight at Harrow. Germany could field three hundred thousand men, trained for battle, with cavalry and artillery, while Britain could land on short notice only twenty thousand men on the continent. If Palmerston attempted to bring France into an alliance with Britain against Germany, then France would undoubtedly demand a piece of Germany—the coveted Rhine provinces—upsetting the balance of Europe even more. Through trade, empire (formal and informal), diplomacy, the navy, and a modicum of force, Britain had shaped much of the world. Britain would still do so, but to a lesser extent. By the 1860s Palmerston faced fewer options. Still confident in spite of the accusation that he was losing his touch, he cheerfully administered the nation and the system of international relations, but with less aplomb and with, for the first time in his career, a noticeable hint of nervousness.

But if Palmerston had fewer options, he nonetheless discerned vague shapes in the misty future. One of his last letters before his death summed up the current tensions and pointed to the changes looming on the horizon. At one level this letter reveals how he managed to put a cheerful face on the advance of Germany against the Duchies, but it also shows how he divined the utility of a rising power like Germany in central Europe to balance an even stronger and more expansionist Russia.

> My dear Russell,—It was dishonest and unjust to deprive Denmark of Sleswig and Holstein. It is another question how those two Duchies, when separated from Denmark, can best be disposed for the best of Europe. I should say that, with that view, it is better that they should to increase [sic] the power of Prussia than that they should form another little state to be added to the cluster of small bodies politic which encumber Germany, and render it of less force that it ought to be in the general balance of power in the world. Prussia is too weak as she

now is ever to be honest or independent in her action; and, with a view to the future, it is desirable that Germany, in the aggregate, should be strong, in order to control those two ambitious and aggressive powers, France and Russia, that press upon her west and east. As to France, we know how restless and aggressive she is, and how ready to break loose for Belgium, for the Rhine, for anything she would be likely to get without too great an exertion. As to Russia, she will, in due time, become a power almost as great as the old Roman Empire. She can become mistress of all Asia, except British India, and whenever she chooses to take it; and when enlightened arrangements shall have made her revenue proportioned to her territory, and railways shall have abridged distances, her command of men will become enormous, her pecuniary means gigantic, and her power of transporting armies over great distances most formidable. Germany ought to be strong in order to resist Russian aggression, and a strong Prussia is essential to German strength. Therefore, though I heartily condemn the whole of the proceedings of Austria and Prussia about the Duchies, I own that I should rather see them incorporated with Prussia than converted into an additional asteroid in the system of Europe.

Foreign affairs took much of Palmerston's attention; Bismarck spoke of settling European conflicts not with diplomacy but with "Blood and Iron." France hoped to expand its borders where it could. Russia steadily filled its huge landmass with an increasingly large population; the Industrial Revolution, slowly moving east, adding a new element that promised in time to turn the eastern bear into a major power. Russian cities began to swell in size, mills and factories producing steel and heavy equipment and railroads connecting a vast land empire together into a single entity and thus easing the movement of troops—making Russia, already a volatile and unpredictable neighbor, even more dangerous to European countries.

Many saw changes coming and advocated altering course after Palmerston's term of office ended. One prominent author, Goldwin Smith, professor of modern history at Oxford University, wrote a series of impassioned letters on the colonies to the *Daily News,* a prominent mass-circulation newspaper. Smith boldly suggested that after Palmerston died the formal empire should be broken up and dissolved. It is interesting that Smith could not bring himself to recommend the implementation of this policy while Palmerston was alive. The prime minister still held the esteem of the public, cheered by crowds as he rode his horse through Hyde Park in his green frock coat. Even as an octogenarian he still made pithy comments in Parliament, and at home in London entertained the British elite with the aged Lady Palmerston sparkling in diamonds at the top of the stairs greeting each visitor by name. When Palmerston gave speeches in Parliament they were still often read aloud from the daily newspapers in pubs and chophouses. Palmerston represented not just a political personality but an age, an epoch of British history itself. After more than a generation of prominence in foreign affairs it is clear why Professor Smith suggested discarding the laurels of empire only after the prime minister's death. The public had come to think of Palmerston as the gentleman version of Britannica, and after so many years in office, Palmerston assumed as much himself. "Old Pam" had become "John Bull." It was unthinkable that any lessening of the imperial role of Britain be undertaken while he stood—visible to taxi drivers from the street—bent over his writing desk late into the night "earning his wages."

Palmerston sensed change in the air. This premonition of diminishing British strength made him less aggressive but more defensive. Missing from earlier decades, the shadow of insecurity slipped silently into Parliament and government offices and became a permanent denizen of the Foreign Office. The need to protect not only the empire but also the homeland became an obsession, and not an unreasonable one. It made Palmerston's tussle with Gladstone, his own Chancellor of the Exchequer, all the more poignant. Gladstone proposed cutting the budget for defense, particularly the training and equipping of 160,00 home volunteers. But the mammoth land powers rising in Europe troubled Palmerston. He particularly worried about an expansionist France, which had begun building ironclad naval vessels. Under these circumstances he was willing to pay the price for security. Gladstone saw extra expenditure as a waste of money, since Britain rested in peace like a ship in port. Economic power, not military might, gave Britain its influence in the world. Cast in a different frame of mind, Palmerston shipped more troops to Canada in 1862 to offset any temptations of the northern states to grab Canada and insisted on a budget that provided increased funds for the army and navy, including the volunteer army. The United States, France, Germany, and Russia all could field armies many times the size of Britain's small force. He wrote to Gladstone,

> There was for a long time an apathetic blindness on the part of the governed and the governors as to the defensive means of the country compared with the offensive means acquired and acquiring by other Powers. The country at last awoke from its lethargy, not indeed to rush into extravagance and uncalled for exertions, but to make up gradually for former omissions, and so far, no doubt, to throw upon a shorter period of time expenses which earlier foresight might have spread over a great length of time.
>
> . . . .We have on the other side of the channel a people who, say what they may, hate us as a nation from the bottom of their hearts, and would make any sacrifice to inflict a deep humiliation upon England. It is natural that this should be so. They are eminently vain, and their passion is glory in war. They cannot forget or forgive Aboukir, Trafalgar, the Peninsula, Waterloo, and St. Helena.

He went on to argue that commercial relations are no replacement for strength. England had the closest economic ties with the northern states that dreamed of a "retaliatory blow upon England" by attacking Canada. Palmerston's letter to his old sparring partner in Parliament, Richard Cobden, unmasked the distrust of human nature behind his defensive posture,

> My dear Mr. Cobden,—I have many apologies to make to you for not having sooner acknowledged the memorandum which you sent me some time ago

suggesting an understanding and agreement between the governments of England and France about the number of ships of war each of the two countries should maintain. It would be very delightful if your Utopia could be realized, and if the nations of the earth would think of nothing but peace and commerce, and would give up quarrelling and fighting altogether. But unfortunately man is a fighting and quarrelling animal; and that this is human nature is proved by the fact that republics, where the masses govern, are far more quarrelsome, and more addicted to fighting than monarchies, which are governed by comparatively few persons. But so long as other nations are animated by these human passions, a country like England, wealthy and exposed to attack, must by necessity be provided with the means of defense, and however expensive these means may be, they are infinitely cheaper than the war which they tend to keep off.

During the last days of office in 1865 the American Civil War ended and the old Parliament had run its term. New elections returned the Liberals, winning 60 percent of the vote, to a majority and increased their seats by thirteen members, for a total of 369 Liberal to 289 Conservative. Of almost a million votes cast, most were "Palmerstonians" voting for "Pam and premier" with the full knowledge that Gladstone, a member of his cabinet, waited in the wings for his chance to assume the helm and lead the nation. Palmerston did not, however, live to see the new Parliament assembled.

Death and Legacy

Over the final year he had spoken less in the house while still attending and keeping up with duties. Gout crippled him in the hands and feet during this period, and he had trouble sleeping. Those closest to him saw death closing in. Palmerston hid the symptoms from others as best he could. Evelyn Ashley described how a few days before his death he sat at breakfast with Lord and Lady Palmerston. Palmerston recounted a story from his school days at Harrow, and he broke into laughter he could not control—very unlike him, and a sign that worried Ashley and Lady Palmerston both. The end came quickly when, out riding his horse, he caught a chill and took to bed with an inflamed kidney. By October, just two days past his eighty-first birthday, he died. His final words, quipped to his physician, "Die? My dear doctor, that is the last thing I shall do." On his desk lay an unfinished letter intended for the next post.

With him flickered out, an early biographer noted, the last candle of the eighteenth century. With his death also died a member that served in the British government from 1807 to 1865, with the exception of only two ministries—those of Peel and Derby. Though he had intended to be buried close to his mother, Queen Victoria ordered a state funeral and his internment in Westminster Abbey with the highest honors.

After his death a logjam of changes broke loose and passed Parliament. Reform was introduced by the Liberals under the leadership of Russell and

Gladstone in 1866, but defeated by the Conservatives who then came to power. Disraeli, the Conservative leader who had long resisted reform, switched sides on the issue to gain an advantage on the Liberals, and in a surprise vote Parliament, with both conservative and radical support, lowered the voting requirements to bring more people into the franchise. Palmerston would have opposed this comprehensive reform that gave more power to the working class. Other reforms came rushing into the national arena after his death, reforms on Ireland and education, for instance. In this sense he had little legacy.

Where then does his legacy lie? His influence can be found in a number of disparate streams. He was in many ways the first modern politician, one who played heavily to the press and the middle classes, to those who went to pubs to drink or who exchanged ideas in clubs and teahouses. He both followed public opinion and at times (a rare feat) managed to change it, as with the Don Pacifico case. To his legacy must be added the doctrine of free trade and the prestige of the British empire in the mid-Victorian period that carried through the decades to the 1930s. Obviously this must be qualified by a few caveats—others supported free trade doctrines, such as Cobden, Bright, and many conservatives as well as liberals. And Britain without Palmerston surely would have peaked in power and prestige during these middle decades of the nineteenth century. But a legacy does not have to be a deposit of original ideas, nor does a legacy consist solely in changing the course of history in a new direction. He had absorbed and he advocated his whole life the ideas of Adam Smith and free trade. He pushed for constitutional governments when he could, though always moderated by his own view of 'balance" between classes and the ideal model of the 1688 Glorious Revolution. By bold and decisive moves—if sometimes flawed and insensitive, he added to the prestige of empire. By advocating free trade and a belief that the world should be open to trade and the changes in governments that followed a rising middle class, he substantially reshaped whole regions of the world.

The empire culturally enriched Britain and added more than just imaginary dash—it changed literature, architecture, patterns of trade, and lured emigrants out and immigrants back in as well. Nor was the empire a superfluous addendum to the Industrial Revolution at home but a world of markets and resources for which Britain's economy was the central hub. Palmerston gave Britain the illusion of always winning, never backing down, always appearing to be in control, appearing—to the nation but often to outsiders as well—to follow the rule of law, bringing other nations to the same standards of fair play and free trade. This was a thin membrane of illusion, a prop to foreign policy that was at times transparent and easily torn. In reality his policy was far more scrupulous, delicate, subtle, and careful. He did not bluster into the 1848 revolutions on the continent; he did not push war with the United States during the Civil War (though he came close), he did not intervene to save the Duchies claimed by the Danes in the 1860s. He fought battles he knew he could win, and this added to the impression of invincibility. His record is one of expansion and imperial construction, formal and informal, when such expansion was feasible. He compromised at all other times. Not all prime ministers who followed Palmerston showed such agility and balance.

Palmerston's longest legacy lies in the extension of free trade, and this in turn aided substantially in the globalization of the world. By kicking in the door of trade in Latin America, the Middle East, Asia, and Africa, he guaranteed that these parts of the world changed forever. They may have entered the web of Western trade and influence eventually, but they entered sooner because of Palmerston, and the changes, and the globalization that have occurred since, are a part of his legacy for good and ill. Forcing China, the Ottomans, and West Africa into trade meant that local culture, tradition, and forms of governments were affected, usually, by compromise and hybrid systems that supported a new collaborative and business class. Palmerston did not start the process of globalization, but his empire of free trade in the nineteenth century, that he did so much to expand, impacted the world in a permanent way. Many disagree that free trade and the globalization that followed have been worth the cultural price. Resistance to empire followed the flag, and that resistance laid the foundation for nationalism, decolonization, and independence.

Imperialism certainly is out of fashion in the current century, at least the open admission of empire. Free trade can also be seen as giving rise to elites that care only about profit, and a ruling class that cares little for the poor, for meaningful culture, or for the greater good. Palmerston, though, may not have disagreed with these critiques; he sought balance between classes and despised the domination of the middle classes over the whole of society. But the "balance" he sought for society in Britain and the world he offered as a cure for capitalism, while avoiding the violence and deculturalization that emerged with radical egalitarianism. Few today would take his cure—there is little popular enthusiasm for a landed elite to give polish and counterweight to the middle classes. But he was a man not only of his time but of our time as well, and that is what makes him so recognizable to contemporaries. He rose to power through privilege, played to public sentiment, and extended the influence and power of his national elite in every part of the world—not unlike prominent leaders of modern democratic and egalitarian societies. He stands out less by his dissimilarity, by his worldly success, and even by his power, than by his impact on the world—a world that would remain structurally unchanged until the middle part of the twentieth century.

A Note on the Sources

The largest holding of papers for Henry John Temple Palmerston is found at the University of Southampton, in Southampton, UK. The Foreign Office records, now housed in the Public Records Office at Kew, still provide the largest scope for the investigation of Palmerston's effect on the world. His many speeches in Parliament are found in *Hansard's Parliamentary Debates*. See also *China Papers 1859–60: Correspondence and Papers relating to China* (Parliamentary papers, 1840); *Insults in China: Correspondence respecting Insults in China* (Parliamentary Papers, 1857); *Levant Papers: Correspondence relative to the Affairs of the Levant* (Parliamentary Papers, 1841); *Opium Papers, Papers relating to the Opium Trade in China 1842–1856* (Parliamentary Papers, 1857); *State Papers: British and Foreign State Papers*, XXIX and LII (London, 1857, 1868).

There are many collections of Palmerston's correspondence with contemporaries. A good place to begin would be Phillip Guedalla, *Gladstone and Palmerston: being the correspondence of Lord Palmerston and with Mr. Gladstone 1851–1865* (London: Victor Gollancz, 1928); Emily Lamb Palmerston, *The Lieven-Palmerston Correspondence, 1828–1856* (London: John Murray, 1943); Kenneth Bourne, *The Letters of the Third Viscount Palmerston to Laurence and Elizabeth Sullivan, 1804–1863* (London: Royal Historical Society, 1979); Brian Connell, ed., *Regina vs. Palmerston: The Correspondence Between Queen Victoria and Her Foreign and Prime Minister, 1837–1865* (London: Evans Brothers, 1961).

A great many biographies on Palmerston have been published since his death. The best collection of letters is found in the biography by Evelyn Ashley, *The Life and Correspondence of Henry Temple, Viscount Palmerston* (London: R. Bentley & son, 1879); H. L. Bulwer and E. Ashley, *Life of Viscount Palmerston,* 5 vols., (London: Bentley, 1871–76). See also Herbert C. F. Bell, *Lord Palmerston* (London: Longman's, 1936); Phillip Guedalla, *Palmerston 1784– 1865* (London: G. P. Putnam's sons, 1927); W. Baring Pemberton, *Lord Palmerston* (London: Batchworth Press, 1954); D. Southgate, *"The Most English Minister . . .": The Policies and Politics of Palmerston* (London: Macmillan, 1966); Kenneth Bourne, *Palmerston: The Early Years, 1781 to 1841* (New York: Macmillan, 1982); and Muriel E. Chamberlain, *Lord Palmerston* (Washington D.C.: The Catholic University of America Press, 1987). The most comprehensive biography to date is Jasper Ridley, Lord Palmerston,

(New York: E. P. Dutton, 1971). A short biography with an exhaustive bibliography of Palmerston primary material can be found in Karen E. Partridge, *Lord Palmerston, 1784–1865: A Bibliography* (Westport, Conn.: Greenwood Press, 1994); Paul R. Ziegler's short biography is designed to introduce readers to the political framework that informed Palmerston's life; see *Palmerston: British History in Perspective* (New York: Palgrave Macmillan, 2003); James Chambers has produced a very readable and sympathetic biography, *Palmerston: The Peoples Darling* (London: John Murray, 2004).

Works about Palmerston's contemporaries are voluminous, but the following are of special interest: George Otto Trevelyan, *The Life and Letters of Lord Macaulay* (New York: Harper & Brothers, 1878); Earl of Malmesbury, *Memoirs of an ex-Minister: an Autobiography* (London: Longman's, 1884); J. Morley, *The Life of Richard Cobden* (London: Macmillan, 1881); Robert Peel, *Sir Robert Peel from his private correspondence,* ed. C. S. Parker (London: John Murray, 1891); Duke of Argyll, *Autobiography and Memoirs,* 2 vols. (London: John Murray, 1907); A. C. Benson ed., *Letters of Queen Victoria, 1837–1861,* 3 vols, (London: John Murray, 1908).

For specialized studies of Palmerston's foreign policy, see A. W. Ward and G. P. Gooch, eds., *Cambridge History of British Foreign Policy 1783–1919,* vol. 2, (Cambridge: Cambridge University Press, 1923); Kingsley Martin, *The Triumph of Lord Palmerston: A Study of Public Opinion in England before the Crimean* (London: Hutchinson, 1963); M. S. Anderson, *The Eastern Question* (London: Macmillan, 1966); David Gillard, *The Struggle for Asia, 1828–1914: A Study in British and Russian Imperialism* (London: Methuen, 1977); Charles Webster, *The Foreign Policy of Palmerston, 1830–1841: Britain, the Liberal Movement and the Eastern Question* (London: Bell, 1951); David F. Government, *Foreign Policy, Domestic Politics, and the Genesis of "Splendid Isolation"* (Ames: Iowa State University Press, 1978); Roger J. Bullen, *Palmerston, Guizot and the Collapse of the Entente Cordiale* (London: Athlone Press, 1974); Keith M. Wilson, ed., *British Foreign Secretaries and Foreign Policy: From Crimean War to First World War* (London: Croom Helm, 1987); David Brown, *Palmerston and the Politics of Foreign Policy, 1846–55* (New York: Manchester University Press, 2002).

For general reference on the age of Palmerston see Llewellyn Woodward, The *Age of Reform, 1815–1870* (Oxford: Clarendon Press, 1963); T. W. Heyck, *The Peoples of the British Isles: A New History: Volume 2: 1688 to 1870* (London: Routledge, Lyceum, 2002); Asa Briggs, *Victorian People: Some Reassessments of People, Institutions, Ideas and Events 1851–1867* (Chicago: University of Chicago Press, 1955); Paul Walter Schroeder, The *Transformation of European Politics, 1763–1848* (Oxford: Clarendon Press, 1994); P. J. Cain and A. G. Hopkins, British *Imperialism: Innovation and Expansion, 1688–1914* (London and New York: Longman, 1993).

Brief Chronology

1784	Henry John Temple Palmerston is born (September 25).
1795–1800	Attends Harrow.
1800–1803	At Edinburgh University under the care of Dugald Stewart.
1802	Father dies and he succeeds to the title, 3rd Viscount Palmerston.
1803–6	Attends Cambridge University.
1805	Mother dies.
1806	Runs for Parliament at Cambridge and is defeated. Runs for Parliament at Horsham and is defeated.
1807	Appointed Junior Lord of the Admiralty. Defeated again for Parliament at Cambridge. Elected to Parliament at Newport.
1809	Becomes Secretary at War.
1812	Reelected to Parliament, this time at Cambridge University.
1813	Gives speech on Catholic Emancipation.
1826	Reelected at Cambridge University. Begins to attract Whig support.
1827	Serves under Canning as Secretary at War.
1829	Visits Paris.
1830	Foreign Secretary in the Whig ministry of Lord Grey.
1831	Deals with numerous policy issues: Belgium, Greece, Italy, Russia, Poland, France, and Portugal. Returned to Parliament at Blechingley.
1832	Reform Bill. Elected at South Hampshire.
1833	Factory Reform Act.
1834	Whig government out of power. Abolition of slavery in British possessions.
1835	Appointed foreign secretary. Elected at Tiverton. Municipal Reform Act.
1837	Victoria becomes queen of England. Rebellion in Canada put down.
1839	Palmerston and Lady Cowper marry.
1841	Palmerston steps down from Foreign Office.
1845	Repeal of the Corn Laws.
1846	Returns to Foreign Office under Russell.
1847	Ten Hours Bill passes Parliament. Irish famine.

1848	Chartist demonstration takes place on Kennington Common.
1850	Blockade of Greece and the Don Pacifico debate.
1851	Palmerston forced out of the Foreign Office for recognizing without consultation the French coup d'état. The Great Exhibition in London.
1852	Palmerston takes on the office of Home Secretary.
1853	Steps down from office of Home Secretary.
1854	Crimean War begins.
1855	Aberdeen defeated, Palmerston becomes prime minister.
1856	The lorcha *Arrow* seized by China.
1857	Palmerston opposed in Parliament for his China policy. New elections return Palmerston to office with large Whig majority. Indian Mutiny. Divorce Bill.
1858	Palmerston resigns from office. British crown takes over India from the East India Company.
1859	Palmerston unites his party and returns as prime minister.
1860	Garibaldi takes Naples. British and French take Peking.
1861	The American Civil War begins. *Trent* incident threatens war between the United States and Britain. Prince Albert dies.
1862	The *Alabama* escapes to sea.
1863	Russia crushes rebellion in Poland. Schleswig-Holstein dispute.
1864	Palmerston and Gladstone differ on further electoral reform.
1865	Palmerston wins election again. Dies October 18.

Index

A

Aberdeen, Lord, 72, 90, 95, 99
Aberdeen administration, 100
Act of Uniformity (1662), 46
Act of Union (1801), 29
Adams, Charles, 115
Africa, 6
Africans, 80–81
Akbar, Emperor, 90
Alabama, 115
Albert, Prince, 85, 93, 104, 110, 114
Albert Memorial, 85
Alexander the Great, 101
Ali, Mehmit, 74–77
Ali, Mohammed, 75
American civil wars, 112–116
"American System," 71
Amristar Massacre (1919), 8
Anglicization of India, 90
Anglo-Persian War of 1856, 101–102
Anglo-Saxons, 87–88
Anti–Corn Law League, 14–15
Antoinette, Marie, 31–32
Argentina, 12, 52, 69–71
Arrow affair, 105–107
Ashely, Anthony. *See* Shaftesbury, Lord
Ashley, Evelyn, 113
Auckland, Lord, 84
Austin, Jane, 23
Australia, 3, 6–7, 87–88, 94, 100

Austria, 48, 50–51, 59, 64–65, 73–74, 93, 101, 110, 112
Azim, Sadr, 101

B

Balmoral Castle, 99
Bangladesh, 87
Battle of Trafalgar in 1805, 48
Battle of Waterloo, 48
Battle of Waterloo in 1815, 98
Beagle, 23
Bedchamber, Lady of the, 57
Belgians, 59–60
Belgium affair, 59–60, 67
Bentham, Jeremy, 17–18, 25–26
    the Bible, 23
Blake, 25
Book of Common Prayer, 46
    boroughs, 61
Brahmins, 90
Brazil, 69–71, 73, 80, 82, 87
Bright, John, 8, 15, 97
Britain, in nineteenth century, 6–7
    art, 25–26
British settlers, 6
    class and society, 18–21
    and Corn Laws, 13–15
    demographic growth, 9–10
    expansion of empire, 8
    free trade, 7, 16–17
    post-Industrial Revolution, 9–13

presence in Asia, 7
religion, 21–23
Romantic movement, 25–26
science, 21–23
as a sea power, 6–7
secularism, 21–23
and "the age of reform," 17–18
women and their role in society,
23–25
Britannia, 6
British empire, during Palmerston era,
2–3, 86–91. *See also* Britain, in
nineteenth century
in Africa, 80–82
decline of power, 118–121
territorial expansion, 87
British identity, 1
British Isles, 87
British "shopocracy," 108
Brunel, Isambard, 1
Buenos Aires, 71–72
Bulwer, Henry, 73, 75
Burke, Edmund, 31–32
Byron, Lord, 25, 53, 97

C

Cain, Peter, 16
Cambridge University, 11, 35
Canada, 3, 7, 49, 87–88, 100, 104, 114,
120
Canning, Lord George, 5, 38, 41–42,
52, 68, 71
Canning, Strafford, 96–97
Cardigan, Lord, 99
Caribbean islands, 87
Carlyle, Thomas, 19, 63
Cartwright, Edmund, 10
"cash nexus," 63
Castlereagh, Lord, 41–42, 50, 60
Catholic Emancipation Act of 1829, 17
Catholic Emancipation measures,
46–47
Cecil, Lord, 67

Celts, 9
Ceylon, 87
Charles X, King, 58
Chartist movement, in Britain, 16, 65,
109
Chile, 70, 73
China, 82–84, 105–107
Chinese exports, 83
Christianity, 6, 21, 23
Church of England, 21–23, 36, 47
Civis Britannica, 90
Clarendon, Lord, 79
Clayton-Bulwer Treaty of 1850, 104
clergy of the Church of England, 21
coal mines, 10
Cobbett, William, 63
Cobden, Richard, 8, 14–15, 68, 97
Co-hong guild, 83
Coleridge, 25
Columbus, Christopher, 104
Combination Acts of 1799–1800, 8
committee on Education in 1839, 17
Conservative Christians, 23
Conservatives, 14–15, 18, 36, 47, 61,
91, 93, 106, 112, 122
Convention of Balta Liman, 75
Corn Laws, 13–15, 20, 90–91
Cowper, Lady, 40, 57
Cowper, Lord, 40
Creole rebellion, 71
Crimean War, 95–99
Cromwell, Oliver, 27
crown colonies, 89
Crystal Palace, 85
cult of Thuggee, 89
Cupid, Lord, 110

D

Dahomey, 81
Danton, 31
Darwin, Charles, 23
Davis, Jefferson, 115

Delancey, General, 43
  del Norte, San Juan, 104
Derby, Lord, 99
  de Rosas, Juan Manuel, 71
  de Rothschild, Lionel, 78
Devon Mining Company, 52
Dickens, Charles, 26
Disraeli, Benjamin, 92, 106, 109, 122
Divorce Act (1857). *See* Matrimonial
  Causes Bill
Dominica, 87
Dominions, 87, 89
Don Pacifico affair, 77–80
Dravidians, 90
Driault, Professor, 75
Dudley, Lord, 53
Duke of Norwalk, 37
Dundas, Sir David, 44–45
Durham Report (1839), 88

E

East Africa, 5, 82
Eastern Question, 73–77
East India Company, 63, 82–83, 88–89
Egg, Augustus, 26
Egypt, 51, 73–77, 82
  electoral reforms, of Palmerston,
    60–62
Elizabeth, 29, 38
Elliot, Captain, 84
El Quebracho, 72
"empire of opinion," 8
Enlightenment, 21
European revolutions of 1848, 65–67
Evangelical revival, 21–22

F

Factory Act of 1833, 17
Factory Act of 1853, 94
Fanny, 29
Fantome, 78

Ferdinand, Emperor, 65
Ferguson, Niall, 2
First War of Independence in India,
  102–103
Fitzharris, Edward, 37
Florence Nightingale, 98, 100
Florida, 115
Forbes, John, 70
France, 6, 10, 27, 31–32, 36, 38, 42,
  47–51, 58–60, 65, 69, 71–72,
  74–75, 77–79, 92, 96, 98, 103,
  113, 118–120
Frederick, King, 66
  free trade, 7, 19, 34
  and Corn Laws, 14
  issues of, 16–17
  philosophy of Palmerston, 67–69
  treaties, 50
French Revolution, 8, 19, 27, 33, 48,
  51, 58, 61, 64

G

Gandhi, 7
Garrick, David, 27
George, David Lloyd, 109
George III, King, 16, 43–44, 47
George IV, King, 16, 52, 54
Georgia, 115
Germany, 10, 13, 35, 58, 60, 116–118,
  120
Gibbon, Edward, 27
Gibbs, Vicary, 37
Gladstone, William, 68, 84, 100,
  107–108, 113, 115
Glorious Revolution of 1688, 46, 48,
  58
Goderich, Viscount, 51, 53
Grattan, Mr., 46
Great Exhibition of 1851, 85
Great Reform Act of 1832, 17
Great Western Railway, 1
Greece, 51, 53–54, 64, 76–79, 97
Greeks, 51, 53–54, 101

Grenada, 87
Grey, Lord, 55–57, 76, 90, 92
    gunboat diplomacy, 82

H

Hare, Francis, 30
Harris, James, 35
Henry, 29
Holmes, Sir Leonard, 37
Holy Alliance, 64, 67
Hopkins, Anthony, 16
House of Commons, 29, 46, 49, 62, 67
House of Lords, 19
Hume, David, 33
    "hungry forties," 13

I

Illicit trade relations, 70
    imperial age of Britain, 2
Indian empire, British ruled, 87–91
Indian Mutiny (1857), 7, 102–103, 107
Industrial Revolution, impact of, 9–13,
    17, 71–72
    agricultural productivity, 9
    demographic growth, 9–10
    economic growth, 11–12
    education, 11
    industrial productivity, 9–10
    influence of British power, 11–12
    iron manufacturing, 9–10
    living conditions, 12
    preconditions for, 9, 11
    and Protestant Reformation, 11
    rail transportation, 12–13
    steam engines, 10, 13
    textiles, 10

J

James Hargreaves' Spinning Jenny, 10
Jenkinson, Robert. *See* Liverpool, Lord
John of Portugal, King, 54

Johnson, Dr. Samuel, 27

K

Kahn, Sir Sayyid Ahmed, 103
Kant, Emmanuel, 17
Katherine, 79
Keats, 25

L

Lagos, 81
Lamb, Emily. *See* Cowper, Lady
La Muette de Portici, 58
    landlords, 19
    and "private act," 28
Lansdowne, Lord, 36
Latin America, informal empire in, 64,
    69–73
Leopold of Saxe-Coburg, Prince, 60
Liberal Party, 112
Lieven, Madame, 97
Light Cavalry Brigade, 99
Lincoln, President, 114
Liverpool, Lord, 45, 47, 50
Louis, Roger, 87
Louis XVI, 31–32
Lunacy Act of 1845, 17
Lyell, Charles, 23
Lyttelton, Lord, 29

M

Macaulay, Thomas, 62, 90
Mahmud II, Sultan, 51
Malmesbury, Lady, 33
Malmesbury, Lord, 37, 42, 66
    marriage law, 107–108
Mary, 29
Mason, James, 114
Matrimonial Causes Bill, 107
Melbourne, Lord, 57, 108
    "memorandum of means," 100
Menshikoff, General, 98–99

mercantile empire, 86–87
"mercantilist" empire, 6
mestizos, 6
Metternich, 65
Mexico, 52, 69, 73, 99
  middle class, 20
Miguel, 54
Mill, John Stuart, 25–26
Mines and Collieries Bill, 92
  modern Britain, 2
  modern citizens of United
    Kingdom, 1
Montevideo citizens, 70, 72
Morning Advertiser, 95
Morris, William, 9
Mosquito Coast conflict, 103–105
Mughal empire, 90
Municipal Corporations Act of 1835,
  17
Murray, James, 72
Museum of Imperial and
  Commonwealth history, Bristol, 1

N

Napoleon, General, 8, 47–49, 74, 82
Napoleonic Wars, 5–6, 8, 47–49, 51,
  69
Napoleon III, Emperor, 90, 96, 101,
  111–112, 117
Nature and Causes of the Wealth of
  Nations (1776), 34
New Brunswick, 87
New Imperialism, 2
Newman, John Henry, 22–23
New Testament Acts, 78
New Zealand, 3, 6–7, 87–88
Nicholas, Russian Czar, 96, 101
Nicholas I, czar of Russia, 66
Niger, 81
Norton, Caroline, 108
Norton, Lord, 108

O

O'Kane, Mrs., 110
Oman, 82
On Liberty, 26
Ontario, 87
  opium trade, 83
Opium War of 1839–42, 84
Ottoman Empire, 73–77, 90, 96–97
  overseas empires, 6
Oxford movement, 22–23
Oxford University, 11, 35

P

Pacifico, David, 77. *See also* Don
  Pacifico affair
Pakistan, 87
Palmerston, Lady, 24, 29, 31–32, 57
Palmerston, Lord
  and American civil wars, 112–116
  and Anglo-Persian War of 1856,
    101–102
  antislavery attitudes in Africa,
    80–82
  Arrow affair, 105–107
  Belgium affair, 59–60, 67
  and Catholic Emancipation meas-
    ures, 46–47
  as Chancellor of the Exchequer,
    41–46
  chauvinist attitude, 63–64
  in China, 82–84
  chronology, 124–125
  and conflict over the Mosquito
    Coast, 103–105
  and Crimean War, 95–99
  death of, 121–122
  and death of father, 34–35
  on divorce, 107–108
  and Don Pacifico affair, 77–80
  electoral reforms, 60–62
  and European revolutions of 1848,
    65–67

evangelical principles of, 39–40
family life, 28–29
foreign policies, 50–51, 93,
    109–110
as foreign secretary, 57–60, 63–65
free trade policies, 50–52, 67–69
and globalization, 67–69
and Indian Mutiny, 102–103
informal empire in Latin America,
    64, 69–73
legacy of, 122–123
life at Harrow, 31
life at St. John's College, 35–36
marriage law, 107–108
as a member of Whig-dominated
    cabinet, 55–56
and Napoleonic Wars, 47–49
Parliament years, 36–41
popularity of, 91–95, 108–112, 117
as prime minister, 99–101
prosecution of brewery workers,
    109–110
relationship with Adam Smith,
    32–36
relationship with Queen Victoria,
    92–94
role in the unification of Italian
    states, 112
schooling, 29–32
as Secretary of Embassy to
    Constantinople, 73–77
sexual scandals, 92–94, 110–111
style of leadership, 66
in Wellington ministry, 53–54
Palmerston, Viscount, 27, 31–32, 35
Parker, Admiral, 79
Parnell, Henry, 8
Pasha, Omar, 96
Pasha of Egypt, 76
Paul, Apostle, 78
Pax Britannica, 90
Peace of Amiens, 48
Peace of Paris, 101

Peel, Robert, 15, 17, 20, 40, 45, 62, 90,
    92, 100
Peers of Ireland, 29
Perceval, Prime Minister Spencer,
    41–42, 45
Peru, 69, 73
Peterloo Massacre (1819), 20
Petty, Lord Henry, 33, 36
Philippe, King Louis, 58–59, 65
Pitt, William, 36
Platte region, 72
Poland, 95
Ponsonby, Lord, 77
Poor Law Amendment Act of 1834,
    17–18
Portland, Lord, 41
    potato crop failure, Ireland, 9, 15
Power Loom, 10
Pragmatism, 59
Pride and Prejudice, 23
Prince Edward Island, 87
Principles of Geology, 23
Prison Act of 1835, 17
Protestant Reformation, 21
Prussia, 48, 51, 60, 64–67, 117–119
Public Health Act of 1845, 17
Pumicestone, Lord, 43
Punch, 92
Puritans, 21

Q

Qajar dynasty, 101
Quebec, 87

R

Raglan, Lord, 98–99
Rappahannock, 115
Reform Act of 1832, 62
    reform acts, 17–18
Repeal of the Test and Corporations
    Acts of 1828, 17
Reynolds, Sir Joshua, 27

Richard Arkwright's Water Frame, 10
Ridley, Jasper, 84
    right of "capitulations," 75
Roman Citizen, 79–80
Roman empire, 79
Roman law, 78
Romantic movement, 25
Rousseau, 21
Royal Commission of Canals, 16
Royal Navy, 77, 81, 84, 92
Royal Society Sir Joseph Banks, 27
Russell, Lord John, 66, 90, 92, 96, 99,
    112–113
Russia, 6, 35, 48, 50–51, 53–56,
    59–60, 64, 66, 74–77, 90–93,
    95–103, 112, 116, 118–120

S

Safavid empire, 101
Samuel Crompton's Spinning Mule, 10
San Jacinto, 114
Scott, Gilbert, 85
Secretary of State for India, 88
Sepoys, 101
Serbs, 74
Shaftesbury, Lord, 94
Shelly, 25
Shenandoah, 115
    slave trade, practice of, 80–82, 87
Slavic nation, 51, 74
Slidell, John, 114
Smith, Adam, 17, 32–36
    society, nineteenth-century, 18–19
Son of Heaven, 107
South Africa, 7, 88
Spanish colonial monopolies, 70
Spanish government, 50
Spanish Marriages, issue of, 90
St. Vincent, 87
Stephenson, George, 13
Stewart, Dugald, 32–33
Sudras, 90

sugar plantations, 87
Syria, 76–77

T

Talleyrand, 59
Tanzania (Tanganyika), 82
Temple, Henry John, 5
Tennyson, 97, 99
Test Act of 1673, 46
Test and Corporations Act (1828), 11
Theory of Moral Sentiments (1759), 33
Thoburn, Bishop J. M., 8
Thompson, James, 6
Times, 95, 100
Tobago, 87
    treaty of Adrianople, 53
    treaty of Commerce and Navigation
        (Oman with Britain), 82
    treaty of Nanking (1842), 84, 105
    treaty of Unkiar Skelessi, 76
Trent, 114
Trevelyan, G. M., 16
Tudor royal family, 27
Turkey, 73, 79, 92, 96, 98. *See also*
    Ottoman Empire
Turkish elites, 51
Turks, 73–77, 97

U

United States, 1–2, 6, 9, 12–13, 39, 45,
    61, 64, 66–67, 69–71, 73, 85–87,
    103–108, 112–116, 120, 122
    upper-class status, 19, 24
    upper-class women, status of,
        23–24
Uruguay, 69–73
Utilitarianism, 17, 25

V

"Viceroy," use of term, 88
Victoria, Queen, 12, 16, 57, 66, 85, 92,
    115

Victorian age, British identity during, 1
Vienna conference, 101
Voltaire, 21
    von Haynau, Baron, 110

W

Walmsley, Sr., J., 106
Watt, James, 13
Wesley, John, 21
Western system of law, 90
Whigs, 15, 17, 22, 33–34, 38, 53
Wilberforce, Samuel, 87, 107
Wilkes, Captain, 114

William, 29, 94
William IV of Prussia, 65
William of Orange, 58–60
Windsor Great Park, 93
    women of Victorian society, 23–25
Wood, Charles, 62
Wordsworth, 25
working class, 20
Wyse, Thomas, 78

Z

Zanzibar, 82